THE DALAI LAMA, A POLICY OF KINDNESS

WINNER OF THE
NOBEL PEACE PRIZE

THE DALAI LAMA,
A POLICY OF KINDNESS

An Anthology of Writings By and About the Dalai Lama

Foreword by Senator Claiborne Pell,
Chairman of the Senate Foreign Relations Committee

Compiled and edited by Sidney Piburn

Snow Lion Publications
Ithaca, New York, USA

Snow Lion Publications
P.O. Box 6483
Ithaca, NY 14851 USA
Tel: 607-273-8519

Printed in the USA

Printing History

First Printing 1990	Ninth Printing 1993
Second Printing 1990	Tenth Printing 1993
Third Printing 1990	Eleventh Printing 1993
Fourth Printing 1991	Twelfth Printing 1995
Fifth Printing 1991	Thirteenth Printing 1996
Sixth Printing 1991	Fourteenth Printing 1996
Seventh Printing 1992	Fifteenth Printing 1997
Eighth Printing 1992	Sixteenth Printing 1998

Also available in these languages:

Korean, Czech, French, German, Portugese, Spanish, Chinese, Russian, Italian, and Japanese.

Library of Congress Cataloging-in-Publication Data

The Dalai Lama, a policy of kindness : an anthology of writings by and about the Dalai Lama / compiled and edited by Sidney Piburn ; foreword by Claiborne Pell.
    p.   cm.
    Includes biographical references.
    ISBN 0-55939-022-0 (Second Edition)
    1. Bstan-'dzin-rgya-mtsho, Dalai Lama XIV, 1934–
I. Piburn, Sidney.
BQ7935.B777D35   1990
294.3'923'092—dc20
    [B]   90-31752
                                     CIP

"Head tilted back and eyes squeezed shut, he bursts into a gale of laughter. . . Like most Tibetans he is gifted with a keen sense of humor, and when he laughs his entire body takes part. He has a wonderful, unembarrassed laugh that begins as a deep-throated roar and fades away on a high pitch, as if all his previous thirteen incarnations were joining in with him. That he is able to laugh in the face of adversity after all he has experienced during the past three decades, suggests that he is a man who has found inner peace."

Michael Goodman

Contents

Foreword

On December 10, 1989, the Norwegian Nobel Committee awarded the Nobel Peace Prize to the 14th Dalai Lama, the religious and political leader of the Tibetan people.

I take particular pleasure in this recognition, as I was among those who nominated the Dalai Lama for this most prestigious award.

It is my hope that the high moral significance of the Nobel Prize with its attendant affirmation of the Dalai Lama's high stature will inspire and empower the Tibetan people and the people of China to pursue, as envisioned by the Dalai Lama, a "Middle Path" to peace, rejecting violence and embracing peaceful resolution through dialogue.

Moreover, I hope that this recognition will focus international attention on the plight and aspirations of the Tibetan people and draw world support for their efforts to save the imperilled Tibetan culture.

In the eighty-eight years of the Nobel Prize's existence, no one has been more deserving than the Dalai Lama, whose life philosophy has been founded upon the concept of universal responsibility and reverence for all living things. His advocacy has included more than human rights. Nature, too, has its rights in his vision of a better world, one that neither the Chinese, nor any other power, can morally violate.

This past year we have witnessed the unfolding of events many believed improbable in our lifetime. We have seen the birth of democracy in nations where human freedoms had been proscriptly denied. We have watched the powerful swell of popular unrest crest to a demand for reform, toppling governments in Poland, East Germany, Czechoslavakia, Bulgaria and Hungary. But the terrible scenes of freedom squelched in Tibet and China remind us that the march of democracy has moved with uneven step.

China will survive these days of repression and political retrogression. We can be less certain about Tibet—hidden from view by restrictive policies and under martial law since March 1989, and, by many accounts, threatened with a massive population transfer of Chinese. Our vigil for peace, reason and freedom in Tibet must never be waiving. We can find great hope in the assuredness that the Dalai Lama will continue to provide us all with a well of wisdom and active counsel for many years to come.

When we look back to the astonishing events of 1989, it is not beyond belief that one day His Holiness the 14th Dalai Lama will be granting audiences in Lhasa. I personally look forward to our meeting there and seeing the 1989 Nobel Peace Prize resting magnificently on the shelves of the Potala Palace.

Senator Claiborne Pell
Chairman of the Senate
Foreign Relations Committee

Introduction

This year the Nobel Prize for Peace was awarded to the Dalai Lama. With this prestigious award His Holiness the Dalai Lama takes his place in the ranks of other leaders whose vision has drawn them into the thick of social struggle.

Although claiming to be only a simple human being, he is known the world over as a tireless worker for peace, a great spiritual teacher, and a man with a gift for conveying great truths in a manner accessible to all. His combination of genuine warmth, infectious sense of humor, penetrating intellect and disarming humility have won him many friends and admirers throughout the world. The Dalai Lama is an extremely complex and multifaceted person. Although he is an astute and accomplished scholar, he is also capable of addressing a general audience with a simplicity and directness which is profound in its intimacy, touching the hearts of his listeners. His life story as well as his own lectures and writings are woven together here to produce a broad portrait of this remarkable man.

Tenzin Gyatso was born into a peasant family in Amdo, eastern Tibet in 1935 and was recognized at the age of two by a government search party and eminent lamas as the fourteenth incarnation in the line of Dalai Lamas. At the age of four he was taken to Lhasa and officially installed as the Dalai Lama.

Following the Chinese invasion and occupation of Tibet in 1950 and the subsequent large scale popular revolt against the Chinese invaders in 1959, the Dalai Lama along with one hundred thousand Tibetan refugees fled across the Himalayas to India and other neighboring countries. In India, he drafted a democratic constitution, formed a Tibetan government-in-exile, and began to establish the institutions that would form the basis for a new Tibetan society: schools, hospitals, orphanages, craft co-ops, farming communitites, institutions for the preservation of traditional music and drama, and monastic institutions. Today, under his leadership, the Tibetans are one of the best-settled refugee groups the world has known.

Tibetan culture is now better preserved *outside* Tibet than *inside*. Inside Tibet the Chinese have, according to the report of the International Commission of Jurists, carried out wholesale cultural genocide. In 1959 there were over six thousand monasteries in Tibet. By 1980, only twelve remained intact. Over one million of Tibet's six million inhabitants have died as a direct result of the Chinese occupation; 87,000 alone in Lhasa (by Chinese count) during the popular uprising in 1959.

In the face of this the Dalai Lama has lost neither hope nor his determination to gain justice for his people. For thirty years he has fought this giant—China—not with anger but with compassion, in a non-violent fashion, armed only with truth. His strategy has been to draw the attention of the world to the plight of the Tibetans in the belief that the justice of their cause will bring about changes in Chinese policy towards Tibet. Long before Tiananmen Square, the Chinese army had repeatedly fired upon unarmed Tibetan demonstrators. After one such brutal attack in March of 1989, when hundreds of Tibetans were killed, martial law was declared in Lhasa—a full three months before Tiananmen Square. Yet even during the Tiananmen Square tragedy newscasters and politicians rarely mentioned Tibet. Even now martial law is still in effect in Lhasa. Although Tibet is roughly the size of Western Europe, the world has largely ignored the suffering that has happened there. Many world political leaders are reluctant to meet publicly with the Dalai Lama for fear of offending the Chinese government.

Tibetans both inside and outside Tibet have long looked to the Dalai Lama for leadership and as the embodiment of their hopes for survival as a people. Because of his remarkable strength of character and advocacy of basic human values independent of a particular political or religious ideology, he is now emerging not only as a leader of the Tibetan people but also as a world leader. During the past thirty years he has worked tirelessly to reshape attitudes for a better society through promoting the importance of kindness and compassion as well as the understanding of our common humanity as a basis for dialogue in the resolution of personal and political conflicts.

This selection of addresses, interviews and biographical essays is intended to convey a picture of the Dalai Lama's personal life, his wide-ranging interests, and his thoughts on issues of global concern. It is hoped that this combination will give the reader who is relatively unfamiliar with the Dalai Lama a deeper appreciation of this man of peace. He emerges as a highly pragmatic man, dedicated to the establishment of non-violent solutions to human problems in the personal, environmental and political arenas. This book is admittedly of an introductory nature. Many of the topics introduced here are explained in much greater detail and depth in other books by the Dalai Lama. A list of his published works is given at the back of this book.

I would like to thank Andrew Harvey, noted author, who originally suggested the idea of this book and urged me to undertake the project. I would also like to thank my friend Jeffrey Cox for his understanding and encouragement, Christine Cox and Susan Kyser for their kind and insightful editorial assistance, Calvin Smith and many other friends who read the manuscript and made useful suggestions, and my wife Yvonne who encouraged me despite my long hours of work and domestic neglect. The assistance of the Nobel Foundation and the many publishers who kindly gave their permission for the use of material included in this anthology is greatly appreciated. Special thanks go to Tenzin Tethong, Special Representative of His Holiness the Dalai Lama, for helping me to acquire transcripts of various talks, and Tenzin Geyche of the Office of His Holiness the Dalai Lama. Most of all I want to express my deepest gratitude to His Holiness the Dalai Lama, Tenzin Gyatso for being an example to us all by showing the way to a better world through his selfless actions as well as through his thought.

Sidney Piburn

1 The Nobel Peace Prize Lecture
Oslo, Norway

Brothers and Sisters:

It is an honor and pleasure to be among you today. I am really happy to see so many old friends who have come from different corners of the world, and to make new friends, whom I hope to meet again in the future. When I meet people in different parts of the world, I am always reminded that we are all basically alike: we are all human beings. Maybe we have different clothes, our skin is of a different color, or we speak different languages. This is on the surface. But basically, we are the same human beings. That is what binds us to each other. That is what makes it possible for us to understand each other and to develop friendship and closeness.

Thinking over what I might say today, I decided to share with you some of my thoughts concerning the common problems all of us face as members of the human family. Because we all share this small planet earth, we have to learn to live in harmony and peace with each other and with nature. That is not just a dream, but a necessity. We are dependent on each other in so many ways that we can no longer live in isolated communities and ignore what is happening outside those communities. We need to help each other when we have difficulties, and we must share the good fortune that we enjoy. I speak to you as just another human being, as a simple monk. If you find what I say useful, then I hope you will try to practice it.

I also wish to share with you today my feelings concerning the plight and aspirations of the people of Tibet. The Nobel Prize is a prize they well deserve for their courage and unfailing determination during the past forty years of foreign occupation. As a free spokesman for my captive countrymen and -women, I feel it is my duty to speak out on their behalf. I speak not with a feeling of anger or hatred towards those who are responsible for the immense suffering of our people and the destruction of our land, homes and culture. They too are human beings who struggle to find happiness and deserve our compassion. I speak to inform you of the sad situation in my country today and of the aspirations of my people, because in our struggle for freedom, truth is the only weapon we possess.

The realization that we are all basically the same human beings, who seek happiness and try to avoid suffering, is very helpful in developing a sense of brotherhood and sisterhood—a warm feeling of love and compassion for others. This, in turn, is essential if we are to survive in this ever-shrinking world we live in. For if we each selfishly pursue only what we believe to be in our own interest, without caring about the needs of others, we not only may end up harming others but also ourselves. This fact has become very clear during the course of this century. We know that to wage a nuclear war today, for example, would be a form of suicide; or that to pollute the air or the oceans, in order to achieve some short-term benefit, would be to destroy the very basis for our survival. As individuals and nations are becoming increasingly interdependent we have no other choice than to develop what I call a sense of universal responsibility.

Today, we are truly a global family. What happens in one part of the world may affect us all. This, of course, is not only true of the negative things that happen, but is equally valid for the positive developments. We not only know what happens elsewhere, thanks to the extraordinary modern communications technology, we are also directly affected by events that occur far away. We feel a sense of sadness when children are starving in Eastern Africa. Similarly, we feel a sense of joy when a family is reunited after decades of separation by the Berlin Wall. Our crops and livestock are contaminated and our health and livelihood threatened when a nuclear accident happens miles away in another country. Our own security is enhanced when peace breaks out between warring parties in other continents.

But war or peace; the destruction or the protection of nature; the violation or promotion of human rights and democratic freedoms; poverty or material well being; the lack of moral and spiritual values or their existence and development; and the breakdown or development of human understanding, are not isolated phenomena that can be analyzed and tackled independently of one another. In fact, they are very much interrelated at all levels and need to be approached with that understanding.

Peace, in the sense of the absence of war, is of little value to someone who is dying of hunger or cold. It will not remove the pain of torture inflicted on a prisoner of conscience. It does not comfort those who have lost their loved ones in floods caused by senseless deforestation in a neighboring country. Peace can only last where human rights are respected, where the people are fed, and where individuals and nations are free. True peace with ourselves and with the world around us can only be achieved through the development of mental peace. The other phenomena mentioned above are similarly interrelated. Thus, for example, we see that a clean environment, wealth or democracy mean little in the face of war, especially nuclear war, and that material development is not sufficient to ensure human happiness.

Material progress is of course important for human advancement. In Tibet, we paid much too little attention to technological and economic development, and today we realize that this was a mistake. At the same time, material development without spiritual development can also cause serious problems. In some countries too much attention is paid to external things and very little importance is given to inner development. I believe both are important and must be developed side by side so as to achieve a good balance between them. Tibetans are always described by foreign visitors as being a happy, jovial people. This is part of our national character, formed by cultural and religious values that stress the importance of mental peace through the generation of love and kindness to all other living sentient beings, both human and animal. Inner peace is the key: if you have inner peace, the external problems do not affect your deep sense of peace and tranquility. In that state of mind you can deal with situations with calmness and reason, while keeping your inner happiness. That is very important. Without this inner peace, no matter how comfortable your life is materially, you may still be worried, disturbed or unhappy because of circumstances.

Clearly, it is of great importance, therefore, to understand the interrelationship among these and other phenomena, and to approach and attempt to solve problems in a balanced way that takes these different aspects into consideration. Of course it is not easy. But it is of little benefit to try to solve one problem if doing so creates an equally serious new one. So really we have no alternative: we must develop a sense of universal responsibility not only in the geographic sense, but also in respect to the different issues that confront our planet.

Responsibility does not only lie with the leaders of our countries or with those who have been appointed or elected to do a particular job. It lies with each of us individually. Peace, for example, starts within each one of us. When we have inner peace, we can be at peace with those around us. When our community is in a state of peace, it can share that peace with neighboring communities, and so on. When we feel love and kindness towards others, it not only makes others feel loved and cared for, but it helps us also to develop inner happiness and peace. And there are ways in which we can consciously work to develop feelings of love and kindness. For some of us, the most effective way to do so is through religious practice. For others it may be non-religious practices. What is important is that we each make a sincere effort to take seriously our responsibility for each other and for the natural environment.

I am very encouraged by the developments which are taking place around us. After the young people of many countries, particularly in northern Europe, have repeatedly called for an end to the dangerous destruction of the environment which was being conducted in the name of economic development, the world's political leaders are now starting to take meaningful steps to address this problem. The report to the United Nations Secretary General by the World Commission on the Environment and Development (the Brundtland report) was an important step in educating governments on the urgency of the issue. Serious efforts to bring peace to war-torn zones and to implement the right to self-determination of some peoples have resulted in the withdrawal of Soviet troops from Afghanistan and the establishment of independent Namibia. Through persistent non-violent popular efforts dramatic changes, bringing many countries closer to real democracy, have occurred in many places, from Manila in the Philippines to Berlin in East Germany. With the Cold War era apparently drawing to a close, people everywhere live with renewed hope. Sadly, the courageous efforts of the Chinese people to bring similar change to their country was brutally crushed last June. But their efforts too are a source of hope. The military might has not extinguished the desire for freedom and the determination of the Chinese people to achieve it. I particularly admire the fact that these young people, who have been taught that "power grows from the barrel of the gun," chose, instead, to use non-violence as their weapon.

What these positive changes indicate is that reason, courage, determination, and the inextinguishable desire for freedom can ultimately win. In the struggle between forces of war, violence and oppression on the one hand, and peace, reason and freedom on the other, the latter are gaining the upper hand. This realization fills us Tibetans with hope that some day we too will once again be free.

The awarding of the Nobel Prize to me, a simple monk from far-away Tibet, here in Norway, also fills us Tibetans with hope. It means that, despite the fact that we have not drawn attention to our plight by means of violence, we have not been forgotten. It also means that the values we cherish, in particular our respect for all forms of life and the belief in the power of truth, are today recognized and encouraged. It is also a tribute to my mentor, Mahatma Gandhi, whose example is an inspiration to so many of us. This year's award is an indication that this sense of universal responsibility is developing. I am deeply touched by the sincere concern shown by so many people in this part of the world for the suffering of the people of Tibet. That is a source of hope not only for us Tibetans, but for all oppressed peoples.

As you know, Tibet has, for forty years, been under foreign occupation. Today, more than a quarter of a million Chinese troops are stationed in Tibet. Some sources estimate the occupation army to be twice this strength. During this time, Tibetans have been deprived of their most basic human rights, including the right to life, movement, speech, worship, only to mention a few. More than one sixth of Tibet's population of six million died as a direct result of the Chinese invasion and occupation. Even before the Cultural Revolution started, many of Tibet's monsteries, temples and historic buildings were destroyed. Almost everything that remained was destroyed during the Cultural Revolution. I do not wish to dwell on this point, which is well documented. What is important to realize, however, is that despite the limited freedom granted after 1979 to rebuild parts of some monasteries and other such tokens of liberalization, the fundamental human rights of the Tibetan people are still today being systematically violated. In recent months this bad situation has become even worse.

If it were not for our community in exile, so generously sheltered and supported by the government and people of India and helped by organizations and individuals from many parts of the world, our nation would today be little more than a shattered remnant of a people. Our culture, religion and national identity would have been effectively eliminated. As it is, we have built schools and monasteries in exile and have created democratic institutions to serve our people and preserve the seeds of our civilization. With this experience, we intend to implement full democracy in a future free Tibet. Thus, as we develop our community in exile on modern lines, we also cherish and preserve our own identity and culture and bring hope to millions of our countrymen and women in Tibet.

The issue of most urgent concern at this time is the massive influx of Chinese settlers into Tibet. Although in the first decades of occupation a considerable number of Chinese were transferred into the eastern parts of Tibet—in the Tibetan provinces of Amdo (Chinghai) and Kham (most of which has been annexed by the neighboring Chinese province)—since 1983 an unprecedented number of Chinese have been encouraged by their government to migrate to all parts of Tibet, including central and western Tibet (which the PRC refers to as the so-called Tibet Autonomous Region). Tibetans are rapidly being reduced to an insignificant minority in their own country. This development, which threatens the very survival of the Tibetan nation, its culture and spiritual heritage, can still be stopped and reversed. But this must be done now, before it is too late.

The new cycle of protest and violent repression, which started in Tibet in September of 1987 and culminated in the imposition of martial law in the capital, Lhasa, in March of this year, was in large part a reaction to this tremendous Chinese influx. Information reaching us in exile indicates that the protest marches and other peaceful forms of protest are continuing in Lhasa and a number of other places in Tibet despite the severe punishment and inhumane treatment given to Tibetans detained for expressing their grievances. The number of Tibetans killed by security forces during the protest in March and of those who died in detention afterwards is not known but is believed to be more than two hundred. Thousands have been detained or arrested and imprisoned, and torture is commonplace.

It was against the background of this worsening situation and in order to prevent further bloodshed, that I proposed what is generally referred to as the Five Point Peace Plan for the restoration of peace and human rights in Tibet. I elaborated on the plan in a speech in Strasbourg last year. I believe the plan provides a reasonable and realistic framework for negotiations with the People's Republic of China. So far, however, China's leaders have been unwilling to respond constructively. The brutal supression of the Chinese democracy movement in June of this year, however, reinforced my view that any settlement of the Tibetan question will only be meaningful if it is supported by adequate international guarantees.

The Five Point Peace Plan addresses the principal and interrelated issues, which I referred to in the first part of this lecture. It calls for (1) Transformation of the whole of Tibet, including the eastern provinces of Kham and Amdo, into a Zone of *Ahimsa* (non-violence); (2) Abandonment of China's population transfer policy; (3) Respect for the Tibetan people's fundamental human rights and democratic freedoms; (4) Restoration and protection of Tibet's natural environment; and (5) Commencement of earnest negotiations on the future status of Tibet and of relations between the Tibetan and Chinese peoples. In the Strasbourg address I proposed that Tibet become a fully self-governing democratic political entity.

I would like to take this opportunity to explain the Zone of Ahimsa or peace sanctuary concept, which is the central element of the Five Point Peace Plan. I am convinced that it is of great importance not only for Tibet, but for peace and stability in Asia.

It is my dream that the entire Tibetan plateau should become a free refuge where humanity and nature can live in peace and in harmonious balance. It would be a place where people from all over the world could come to seek the true meaning of peace within themselves, away from the tensions and pressures of much of the rest of the world. Tibet could indeed become a creative center for the promotion and development of peace.

The following are key elements of the proposed Zone of Ahimsa:

—the entire Tibetan plateau would be demilitarized;

—the manufacture, testing, and stockpiling of nuclear weapons and other armaments on the Tibetan plateau would be prohibited;

—the Tibetan plateau would be transformed into the world's largest natural park or biosphere. Strict laws would be enforced to protect wildlife and plant life; the exploitation of natural resources would be carefully regulated so as not to damage relevant ecosystems; and a policy of sustainable development would be adopted in populated areas;

—the manufacture and use of nuclear power and other technologies which produce hazardous waste would be prohibited;

—national resources and policy would be directed towards the active promotion of peace and environmental protection. Organizations dedicated to the furtherance of peace and to the protection of all forms of life would find a hospitable home in Tibet;

—the establishment of international and regional organizations for the promotion and protection of human rights would be encouraged in Tibet.

Tibet's height and size (the size of the European Community), as well as its unique history and profound spiritual heritage make it ideally suited to fulfill the role of a sanctuary of peace in the strategic heart of Asia. It would also be in keeping with Tibet's historical role as a peaceful Buddhist nation and buffer region separating the Asian continent's great and often rival powers.

In order to reduce existing tensions in Asia, the President of the Soviet Union, Mr. Gorbachev, proposed the demilitarization of Soviet-Chinese borders and their transformation into a "frontier of peace and good-neighborliness." The Nepal government had earlier proposed that the Himalayan country of Nepal, bordering on Tibet, should become a zone of peace, although that proposal did not include demilitarization of the country.

For the stability and peace of Asia, it is essential to create peace zones to separate the continent's biggest powers and potential adversaries. President Gorbachev's proposal, which also included a complete Soviet troop withdrawal from Mongolia, would help to reduce tension and the potential for confrontation between the Soviet Union and China. A true peace zone must, clearly, also be created to separate the world's two most populous states, China and India.

The establishment of the Zone of Ahimsa would require the withdrawal of troops and military installations from Tibet, which would enable India and Nepal also to withdraw troops and military installations from the Himalayan regions bordering Tibet. This would have to be achieved by international agreements. It would be in the best interest of all states in Asia, particularly China and India, as it would enhance their security, while reducing the economic burden of maintaining high troop concentrations in remote areas.

Tibet would not be the first strategic area to be demilitarized. Parts of the Sinai peninsula, the Egyptian territory separating Israel and Egypt, have been demilitarized for some time. Of course, Costa Rica is the best example of an entirely demilitarized country.

Tibet would also not be the first area to be turned into a natural preserve or biosphere. Many parks have been created throughout the world. Some very strategic areas have been turned into natural "peace parks." Two examples are the La Amistad park, on the Costa Rica-Panama border and the Si A Paz project on the Costa Rica-Nicaragua border.

When I visited Costa Rica earlier this year, I saw how a country can develop successfully without an army, to become a stable democracy committed to peace and the protection of the natural environment. This confirmed my belief that my vision of Tibet in the future is a realistic plan, not merely a dream.

Let me end with a personal note of thanks to all of you and

our friends who are not here today. The concern and support which you have expressed for the plight of the Tibetans has touched us all greatly, and continues to give us courage to struggle for freedom and justice; not through the use of arms, but with the powerful weapons of truth and determination. I know that I speak on behalf of all the people of Tibet when I thank you and ask you not to forget Tibet at this critical time in our country's history. We too hope to contribute to the development of a more peaceful, more humane and more beautiful world. A future free Tibet will seek to help those in need throughout the world, to protect nature, and to promote peace. I believe that our Tibetan ability to combine spiritual qualities with a realistic and practical attitude enables us to make a special contribution in however modest a way. This is my hope and prayer.

In conclusion, let me share with you a short prayer which gives me great inspiration and determination:

For as long as space endures,
And for as long as living beings remain,
Until then may I, too, abide
To dispel the misery of the world.

Thank you.

2 Tibet's Living Buddha
by Pico Iyer

Dogs bark in the Himalayan night. Lights flicker across the hillside. On a pitch-black path framed by pines and covered by a bowl of stars, a few ragged pilgrims shuffle along, muttering ritual chants. Just before dawn, as the snowcaps behind take on a deep pink glow, the crowd that has formed outside the three storey Namgyal Temple in northern India falls silent. A strong, slightly stooping figure strides in, bright eyes alertly scanning the crowd, smooth face breaking into a broad and irrepressible smile. Followed by a group of other shaven-headed monks, all of them in claret robes and crested yellow hats, the newcomer clambers up to the temple roof. There, as the sun begins to rise, his clerics seated before him and the solemn, drawn-out summons of long horns echoing across the valley below, the Dalai Lama leads a private ceremony to welcome the Year of the Earth Dragon.

On the second day of Losar, the Tibetan New Year, the man who is a living Buddha to roughly fourteen million people gives a public audience. By eight A.M. the line of petitioners stretches for half a mile along the winding mountain road outside his airy bungalow—leathery mountain men in gaucho hats, long-haired Westerners, little girls in their prettiest silks, all the six thousand residents of the village and thousands more. Later, thirty dusty visitors just out of Tibet crowd inside and, as they set eyes on their exiled leader for the first time in almost three decades, fill the small room with racking sobs and sniffles. Through it all, Tenzin Gyatso, the absolute spiritual and temporal ruler of Tibet, incarnation of the Tibetan god of compassion and fourteenth Dalai Lama in a line that stretches back 597 years, remains serene.

In Tibet, he explains later, Losar used to be conducted on the roof of the thirteen storey Potala Palace, with cookies laid out for the masses. "Every year I used to be really worried when the people rushed to grab the cookies. First, that the old building would collapse, and second, that someone would fall over the edge. Now,"—the rich baritone breaks into a hearty chuckle—"now things are much calmer."

It was twenty-nine years ago last week that the Tibetan uprising against China's occupying forces propelled the Dalai Lama into Indian exile. Yet the spirit of his ancient, fairy-tale theocracy is still very much alive in Dharamsala, a former British hill station 250 miles north of New Delhi. Here, attended by a State Oracle, a rainmaking lama, various medicine men, astrologers and a four-man Cabinet, the Dalai Lama, at fifty-two, incarnates all he has done since first ascending the Lion Throne in Lhasa at age four.

Yet even as the "Protector of the Land of Snows" sustains all the secret exoticism of that otherworldly kingdom reimagined in the West as Shangri-La, he remains very much a leader in the real world. Since the age of fifteen, he has been forced to deal with his people's needs against the competing interests of Beijing, Washington and New Delhi. That always inflammatory situation reached a kind of climax last fall, when Tibetans rioted in Lhasa, their Chinese rulers killed as many as thirty-two people, the Dalai Lama held his first major press conference in Dharamsala, and the U.S. Senate unanimously condemned the Chinese actions. Riots have erupted in recent weeks, but even before that, the modest man in monk's raiment had found himself not only the spiritual symbol linking 100,000 Tibetans in exile to the six million still living under Chinese rule, but also, more than ever, a political rallying point. "The Fourteenth Dalai Lama may be the most popular Dalai Lama of all," he says smiling merrily. "If the Chinese had treated the Tibetans like real brothers, then the Dalai Lama might not be so popular. So,"—he twinkles impishly—"all the credit goes to the Chinese!"

On paper, then, the Dalai Lama is a living incarnation of a Buddha, the hierarch of a government-in-exile and a doctor of metaphysics. Yet the single most extraordinary thing about him may simply be his sturdy, unassuming humanity. The Living God is, in his way, as down to earth as the hardy brown oxfords he wears under his monastic robes, and in his eyes is still the mischief of the little boy who used to give his lamas fits with his invincible skills at hide-and-seek. He delights in tending his flower gardens, looking after wild birds, repairing watches and transistors and, mostly, just meditating. And even toward those who have killed up to 1.2 million of his people and destroyed 6,254 of his monasteries, he remains remarkably forbearing. "As people who practice the Mahayana Buddhist teaching, we pray every day to develop some kind of unlimited altruism," he says. "So there is no point in developing hatred for the Chinese. Rather, we should develop respect for them and love and compassion."

The Fourteenth God-King of Tibet was born in a cowshed in the tiny farming village of Takster in 1935. When he was two, a search party of monks, led to his small home by a corpse that seemed to move, a lakeside vision and the appearance of auspicious cloud formations, identified him as the new incarnation of Tibet's patron god. Two years later, after passing an elaborate battery of tests, the little boy was taken amid a caravan of hundreds into the capital of Lhasa, "Home of the Gods." There he had to live alone with his immediate elder brother in the cavernous thousand-chamber Potala Palace and undertake an eighteen-year course in Metaphysics. By the age of seven, he was receiving envoys from President Franklin

Roosevelt and leading prayers before twenty thousand watchful monks; yet he remained a thoroughly normal little boy who loved to whiz around the holy compound in a pedal car and instigate fights with his siblings. "I recall one summer day—I must have been about seven—when my mother took me to the Norbulingka Summer Palace to see His Holiness," recalls the Dalai Lama's youngest brother Tenzin Choegyal. "When we got there, His Holiness was watering his plants. The next thing I knew, he was turning the hose on me!"

It was at this time too that the precocious boy first displayed his prodigious gift for things scientific, teaching himself the principles of the combustion engine and fixing the palace's generator whenever it went on the blink. To satisfy his insatiable curiosity about a world he was permitted to glimpse only through the silk-fringed curtains of his golden palanquin, the young ruler set up a projector by which he eagerly devoured Tarzan movies, *Henry V* and, best of all, home movies of his own capital. Often, he recalls, he would take a telescope onto the palace roof and wistfully gaze at the boys and girls of Lhasa carelessly going about their lives.

In 1950 the isolation of the "Wish-Fulfilling Gem" and his mountain kingdom was shattered as the Chinese attacked from eight different directions. Suddenly the teenage ruler was obliged to take a crash course in statesmanship, traveling to Beijing to negotiate with Zhou Enlai and Mao Zedong. Finally, in March 1959, when a bloody confrontation seemed imminent as thirty thousand steadfast Tibetans rose up against Chinese rule, the Dalai Lama slipped out of his summer palace dressed as a humble soldier and set off across the highest mountains on earth. Two weeks later, suffering from dysentery and on the back of a dzo, a hybrid yak, the "Holder of the White Lotus" rode into exile in India.

Since then, his has been a singularly delicate balancing act, the guest of a nation that would prefer him to remain silent and the enemy of a nation that much of the world is trying to court. Undeterred, the Dalai Lama has organized fifty-three Tibetan settlements in India and Nepal and set up institutes to preserve his country's arts, its scriptures and its medical traditions. In recent years he has begun to race around the world like a Buddhist John Paul II—lecturing at Harvard, meeting the Pope and attending to his flock, be they unlettered peasants or the American actor Richard Gere (a student of Buddhism since 1982). Always inclined to see the good in everything, he feels that exile has in some respects been a blessing. "When we were in Tibet, there were certain ceremonial activities that took up a lot of time, but the substance was—not much. All those exist no longer. That's good, I think. Also, because we are refugees, we have become much more realistic. There's no point now in pretending."

Many young Tibetans would like their leader to be more militant. Angrily noting that there are more than three thousand political prisoners in central Tibet alone and that Beijing has at least three hundred thousand troops on the "Rooftop of the World," they advocate violence. But the Dalai Lama refuses to be intemperate. "Once your mind is dominated by anger," he notes thoughtfully, "it becomes almost mad. You cannot take right decisions, and you cannot see reality. But if your mind is calm and stable, you will see everything exactly as it is. I think all politicians need this kind of patience. Compared with the previous Soviet leaders, for example, Gorbachev, I think, is much more calm. Therefore, more effective."

Pacifism, however, does not mean passivity. "Ultimately," he continues, "the Chinese have to realize that Tibet is a separate country. If Tibet was always truly a part of China, then, whether Tibetans liked it or not, they would have to live with it. But that's not the case. So we have every right to demand our rights."

The Dalai Lama spends much of his time reflecting on how Tibetan Buddhism can teach, and learn from, other disciplines. He believes, for example, that Buddhism can show Marxism how to develop a genuine socialist ideal "not through force, but through reason, through a very gentle training of the mind, through the development of altruism." He sees many points of contact between his faith and psychology, cosmology, neurobiology, the social sciences and physics. There are many thing we Buddhists should learn from the latest scientific findings. And scientists can learn from Buddhist explanations. We must conduct research, and then accept the results. If they don't stand up to experimentation," he says, beaming subversively, "Buddha's own words must be rejected."

Such quiet radicalism has at times unsettled followers so devout that they would readily give up their lives for their leader. In the draft constitution he drew up in 1963, the God-King included, against his people's wishes, a clause that would allow for his impeachment. Now he is considering new methods for choosing the next Dalai Lama—adopting an electoral system similar to the Vatican's, perhaps, or selecting on the basis of seniority, or even dispensing with the entire institution. "I think the time has come—not necessarily to take a decision very soon, but to start a more formal discussion, so that people can prepare their minds for it."

In the meantime, the exiled leader will continue to pursue a simple, selfless life that is close to the Buddhist ideal of the Middle Way—neither hostile to the world nor hostage to it. Buddhism's supreme living deity still refuses to fly first class and thinks of himself always, as he told the press last fall, as a "simple Buddhist monk." Though he is one of the most erudite scholars of one of the most cerebral of all the world's philosophies, he has a gift for reducing his doctrine to a core of lucid practicality, crystallized in the title of his 1984 book, *Kindness, Clarity and Insight* (Snow Lion Publications). "My true religion," he has said, "is kindness."

It is, in fact, the peculiar misfortune of the Chinese to be up against one of those rare souls it is all but impossible to dislike. Beijing has felt it necessary to call him a "political corpse, bandit and traitor," a "red-handed butcher who subsisted on people's flesh." Yet everyone who meets the Dalai Lama is thoroughly disarmed by his good-natured warmth and by a charisma all the stronger for being so gentle.

To an outsider, the life of a living Buddha can seem a profoundly lonely one. In recent years, moreover, nearly all the people closest to the Tibetan ruler—his senior tutor, his junior tutor, his mother and the elder brother who in youth was his only playmate—have died. Yet this, like everything else, the Dalai Lama takes, in the deepest sense, philosophically. "Old friends pass away, new friends appear," he says with cheerful matter-of-factness. "It's just like the days. An old day passes, a new day arrives. The important thing is to make it meaningful: a meaningful friend—or a meaningful day."

3 His Life
An Interview by John Avedon

JA: What were your first feelings on being recognized as the Dalai Lama? What did you think had happened to you?

DL: I was very happy. I liked it a lot. Even before I was recognized, I often told my mother that I was going to go to Lhasa. I used to straddle a window sill in our house pretending that I was riding a horse to Lhasa. I was a very small child at the time, but I remember this clearly. I had a strong desire to go there. Another thing I didn't mention in my autobiography is that after my birth, a pair of crows came to roost on the roof of our house. They would arrive each morning, stay for a while and then leave. This is of particular interest as similar incidents occurred at the birth of the First, Seventh, Eighth and Twelfth Dalai Lamas. After their births, a pair of crows came and remained. In my own case, in the beginning, nobody paid attention to this. Recently, however, perhaps three years ago, I was talking with my mother, and she recalled it. She had noticed them come in the morning, depart after a time, and then the next morning come again. Now, the evening after the birth of the First Dalai Lama, bandits broke into the family's house. The parents ran away and left the child. The next day when they returned and wondered what had happened to their son, they found the baby in a corner of the house. A crow stood before him, protecting him. Later on, when the First Dalai Lama grew up and developed in his spiritual practice, he made direct contact during meditation with the protective deity, Mahakala. At this time, Mahakala said to him, "Somebody like you who is upholding the Buddhist teaching needs a protector like me. Right on the day of your birth, I helped you." So we can see, there is definitely a connection between Mahakala, the crows, and the Dalai Lamas.

Another thing that happened, which my mother remembers very clearly, is that soon after I arrived in Lhasa, I said that my teeth were in a box in a certain house in the Norbulinka. When they opened the box, they found a set of dentures which had belonged to the Thirteenth Dalai Lama. I pointed to the box, and said that my teeth were in there, but right now I don't recall this at all. The new memories associated with this body are stronger. The past has become smaller, more vague. Unless I made a specific attempt to develop such a memory, I don't recall it.

JA: Do you remember your birth or the womb state before?

DL: At this moment, I don't remember. Also, I can't recall if at that time when I was a small child, I could remember it. However, there was one slight external sign perhaps. Children are usually born with their eyes closed. I was born with my eyes open. This may be some slight indication of a clear state of mind in the womb.

JA: When you were a little boy, how did you feel on being treated by adults as an important person? Were you apprehensive or even frightened at being so revered?

DL: Tibetans are very practical people. Older Tibetans would never treat me that way. Also, I was very self-confident. When I first approached Lhasa on the Debuthang plain, the Nechung

Oracle came to further verify that I was the correct choice. With him came an old, very respected, and highly realized *geshay* from Loseling College of Drepung Monastery. He was deeply concerned whether or not I was the correct choice. To have made a mistake in finding the Dalai Lama would be very dangerous. Now he was a religious man—not someone in the government. He came into the tent where I was in a group audience, and determined that unquestionably I was the right choice. So you see, though there were certain very proper old people who wanted to be sure, I apparently put on a good performance and convinced them (laughter). I was never uneasy in my position. Charles Bell has mentioned that I was taking it all quite casually. To do with fear, there's one thing I remember clearly. One night I wanted to go visit my mother, who had come with the rest of my family to Lhasa. I was in the tent of the regent. A very large bodyguard was standing by the entrance. It was evening, sunset, and this man had a bad, damaged eye. I remember being scared, frightened then, to go out of the tent.

JA: Between the ages of sixteen and eighteen, after you assumed temporal power, did you change?

DL: Yes, I changed. . .a little bit. I underwent a lot of happiness and pain. Within that and from growing, gaining more experience, from the problems that arose and the suffering, I changed. The ultimate result is the man you see now (laughter).

JA: How about when you just entered adolescence? Many people have a difficult time defining themselves as an adult. Did this happen to you?

DL: No. My life was very much in a routine. Two times a day I studied. Each time I studied for an hour, and then spent the rest of the time playing (laughter). Then at the age of 13, I began studying philosophy, definitions, debate. My study increased, and I also studied calligraphy. It was all in a routine though, and I got used to it. Sometimes, there were vacations. These were very comfortable; happy. Losang Samten, my immediate elder brother, was usually at school, but during these times he would come to visit. Also, occasionally my mother would bring special bread from our province of Amdo. Very thick and delicious. She made this herself.

JA: Did you have an opportunity to have a relationship with your father when you were growing up?

DL: My father died when I was 13.

JA: Are there any of your predecessors in whom you have a special interest or with whom you have a particular affinity?

DL: The Thirteenth Dalai Lama. He brought a lot of improvement to the standards of study in the monastic colleges. He gave great encouragement to the real scholars. He made it impossible for people to go up in the religious heirarchy, becoming an abbot and so forth, without being totally qualified. He was very strict in this respect. He also gave tens of thousands of monks ordinations. These were his two main religious achievements. He didn't give many initiations, or many lectures. Now, with respect to the country, he had great thought and consideration for statecraft—the outlying districts in particular—how they should be governed and and so forth. He cared very much about how to run the government more efficiently. He had great concern about our borders and that type of thing.

JA: During the course of your own life, what have been your greatest personal lessons or internal challenges? Which realizations and experiences have had the most effect on your growth as an individual?

DL: Regarding religious experience, some understanding of *shunya* [emptiness: lack of independent self-nature]—some feeling, some experience—and mostly *bodhichitta*, altruism. It has helped a lot. In some ways, you could say that it has made me into a new person, a new man. I'm still progressing. Trying. It gives you inner strength, courage, and it is easier to accept situations. That's one of the greatest experiences.

JA: On the bodhichitta side, are you speaking about a progressive deepening of realization or a certain moment associated with external experience?

DL: Mainly internal practice. There could also be external causes or circumstances. External factors could have played a part in the development of some feeling for bodhichitta. But mainly, it has to come from internal practice.

JA: Can you cite a specific moment from your practice when you crossed a threshold?

DL: Regarding shunya theory, first shunya theory, then bodhichitta feeling... Around '65, '66, in that period. This is really a personal matter. For a true religious practitioner, these things must be kept private.

JA: OK. Not asking you about your own deepest experience, but in terms of the course of your life—the events of your life—how have these affected you as a man? How have you grown through experiencing them?

DL: Being a refugee has been very useful. You are much closer to reality. When I was in Tibet as the Dalai Lama, I was trying to be realistic, but somehow because of circumstances, there was some distance, I think. I was a bit isolated from the reality. I became a refugee. Very good. So there was a good opportunity to gain experience and also determination or inner strength.

JA: When you became a refugee, what helped you gain this strength? Was it the loss of your position and country, the fact of everyone suffering around you? Were you called on to lead your people in a different way than you had been accustomed to?

DL: Being a refugee is a really desperate, dangerous situation. At that time, everyone deals with reality. It is not the time to pretend things are beautiful. That's something. You feel involved with reality. In peace time, everything goes smoothly. Even if there is a problem, people pretend that things are good.

During a dangerous period, when there's a dramatic change, then there's no scope to pretend that everything is fine. You must accept that bad is bad. Now when I left the Norbulinka, there was danger. We were passing very near the Chinese military barracks. It was just on the other side of the river, the Chinese checkpost there. You see, we had definite information two or three weeks before I left, that the Chinese were fully prepared to attack us. It was only a question of the day and hour.

JA: At that moment, when you crossed the Kyichu River and met the party of Khamba guerillas waiting for you, did you assume a direct leadership capacity? Who, for instance, made the decisions on your flight?

DL: As soon as we left Lhasa, we set up an inner group, a committee to discuss each point. Myself and eight other people.

JA: Was it your idea to make it unanimous?

DL: Yes. Those who were left behind in Lhasa also established a People's Committee. Something like a revolutionary council. Of course, from the Chinese viewpoint, this was a counter revolutionary committee. Chosen by the people, you see, within a few days...They set up that committee and all major decisions were made by it. I also sent a letter to that committee, certifying it. In our small committee, those who were escaping with me, we discussed the practical points each night. Originally, our plan was to establish our headquarters in southern Tibet, as you know. Also, I mentioned to Pandit Nehru—I think on the 24th of April, 1959—that we had established a Tibetan temporary government, shifted from Lhasa to southern Tibet. I mentioned this casually to the Prime Minister. He was sightly agitated (laughter). ''We are not going to recognize your government,'' he said. Although this government had been formed while still inside Tibet, and I was already in India....

JA: I'd like to ask you about being the incarnation of the bodhisattva of infinite compassion, *Avalokiteshvara* [Tibetan: *Chenrezi*]. How do you personally feel about this? Is it something you have an unequivocal view of one way or another?

DL: It is difficult for me to say definitely. Unless I engaged in a meditative effort, such as following my life back breath by breath, I couldn't say exactly. We believe that there are four types of rebirth. One is the common type, wherein a being is helpless to determine his or her rebirth, but only incarnates in dependence on the nature of past actions. The opposite is that of an entirely enlightened Buddha, who simply manifests a physical form to help others. In this case, it is clear that the person is a Buddha. A third is one who, due to past spiritual attainment, can choose, or at least influence, the place and situation of rebirth. The fourth is called a blessed manifestation. In this the person is blessed beyond his normal capacity to perform helpful functions, such as teaching religion. For this last type of birth, the person's wishes in previous lives to help others must have been very strong. They then obtain such empowerment. Though some seem more likely than others, I cannot definitely say which I am.

JA: From the viewpoint then of the realistic role you play as Chenrezi, how do you feel about it? Only a few people have been considered, in one way or another, divine. Is the role a burden or a delight?

DL: It is very helpful. Through this role I can be of great benefit to people. For this reason I like it: I'm at home with it. It's clear that it is very helpful to people, and that I have the karmic relationship to be in this role. Also, it is clear that there is a karmic relationship with the Tibetan people in particular. Now you see, you may consider that under the circumstances, I am very lucky. However, behind the word luck, there are actual causes or reasons. There is the karmic force of my ability to assume this role as well as the force of my wish to do so. In regard to this, there is a statement in the great Shantideva's *Engaging in the Bodhisattva Deeds* which says, "As long as space exists, and as long as there are migrators in cyclic existence, may I remain—removing their suffering." I have that wish in this lifetime, and I know I had that wish in past lifetimes.

JA: With such a vast goal as your motivation, how do you deal with your personal limitations, your limits as a man?

DL: Again, as it says in Shantideva, "If the blessed Buddha cannot please all sentient beings, then how could I?" Even an enlightened being, with limitless knowledge and power and the wish to save all others from suffering, cannot eliminate the individual karma of each being.

JA: Is this what keeps you from being overwhelmed when you see the suffering of the six million Tibetans, who on one level, you are responsible for?

DL: My motivation is directed towards all sentient beings. There is no question, though, that on a second level, I am directed towards helping Tibetans. If a problem is fixable, if a situation is such that you can do something about it, then there is no need to worry. If it's not fixable, then there is no help in worrying. There is no benefit in worrying whatsoever.

JA: A lot of people say this, but few really live by it. Did you always feel this way, or did you have to learn it?

DL: It is developed from inner practice. From a broader perspective, there will always be suffering. On one level, you are bound to meet with the effects of the unfavorable actions you yourself have previously committed in either body, speech or mind. Then also, your very own nature is that of suffering. There's not just one factor figuring into my attitude, but many different ones. From the point of view of the actual entity producing the suffering, as I have said, if it is fixable, then there is no need to worry. If not, there is no benefit to worrying. From the point of view of the cause, suffering is based on past unfavorable actions accumulated by oneself and no other. These karmas are not wasted. They will bear their fruit.

One will not meet with the effects of actions that one has not done oneself. Finally, from the viewpoint of the nature of suffering itself, the aggregates of the mind and body have as their actual nature, suffering. They serve as a basis for suffering. As long as you have them you are susceptible to suffering. From a deep point of view, while we don't have our independence and are living in someone else's country, we have a certain type of suffering, but when we return to Tibet and gain our independence, then there will be other types of suffering. So, this is just the way it is. You might think that I'm pessimistic, but I am not. This is the Buddhist realism. This is how, through Buddhist teaching and advice, we handle situations. When fifty thousand people in the Shakya clan were killed one day, Shakyamuni Buddha, their clansman, didn't suffer at all. He was leaning against a tree, and he was saying, "I am a little sad today because fifty thousand of my clansmen were killed." But he, himself, remained unaffected. Like that, you see (laughter). This was the cause and effect of their own karma. There was nothing he could do about it. These sorts of thoughts make me stronger; more active. It is not at all a case of losing one's strength of mind or will in the face of the pervasive nature of suffering.

JA: I'm interested in what you do to relax: gardening and experimenting with electronics.

DL: Oh, my hobbies. Passing time (laughter). When I can repair something, it gives me real satisfaction. I began dismantling things when I was young because I was curious about how certain machines functioned. I wanted to know what was inside the motor, but these days I only try to fix something when it breaks.

JA: And gardening?

DL: Gardening in Dharamsala is almost a hopeless thing. No matter how hard you work, the monsoon comes and destroys everything. You know, a monk's life is very gratifying; very happy. You can see this from those who have given up the robes. They definitely know the value of monkhood. Many have told me how complicated and difficult life is without it. With a pretty wife and children you might be happy for some time. In the long run, though, many problems naturally come about. Half of your independence—your freedom—is lost. If there is some benefit or meaning to experiencing the trouble which arises on giving up your independence, then it is worthwhile. If it is an effective situation which helps people, then it is good. The trouble becomes worthwhile. But if it isn't, it is not worthwhile.

JA: But none of us would even be here talking about this unless we had mothers and fathers!

DL: I'm not saying that having children is bad, or that everyone should be a monk. Impossible (laughter).

I think that if one's life is simple, contentment has to come. Simplicity is extremely important for happiness. Having few desires, feeling satisfied with what you have is very vital. There are four causes which help produce a superior being. Satisfaction with whatever food you get. Satisfaction with rags for clothing, or acceptance of any covering—not wishing for fancy or colorful attire. Satisfaction with just enough shelter to protect yourself from the elements. And finally, an intense delight in abandoning faulty states of mind and in cultivating helpful ones in meditation.

4 A Life in the Day: The Dalai Lama

As told to Vanya Kewley

When I wake at four o'clock, I automatically start reciting the *Ngagjhinlab* mantra. It's a prayer that dedicates everything I do, my speech, my thoughts, my deeds, my whole day, as an offering, a positive way to help others. Like all monks, I obey a vow of poverty, so there are no personal possessions. My bedroom has just a bed and the first thing I see when I wake is the face of the Buddha on a holy seventeenth-century statue from Kyirong, one of the very few that escaped the Chinese desecration. It's cold when I wake, as we are at 7000 feet, so I do some exercises, wash and dress quickly.

I wear the same maroon robe as all the monks. It's not of good quality, and it's patched. If it was of good material and in one piece, you could sell it and gain something. This way you can't. This reinforces our philosophy of becoming detached from worldly goods. I meditate until five-thirty and make prostrations. We have a special practice to remind ourselves of our misdeeds and I make my confession and recite prayers for the well-being of all sentient beings.

Then at daybreak, if the weather is fine, I go into the garden. This time of day is very special to me. I look at the sky. It's very clear and I see the stars and have this special feeling— of my insignificance in the cosmos. The realization of what we Buddhists call impermanence. It's very relaxing. Sometimes I don't think at all and just enjoy the dawn and listen to the birds.

Then Penjor or Loga, monks from Namgyal monastery who have been with me for 28 years, bring my breakfast. It's a half-Tibetan, half-Western mixture. *Tsampa*—roasted barley flour— and porridge. While I have breakfast, my ears are very busy listening to the news on the BBC World Service.

Then at about six, I move into another room and meditate until nine. Through meditation, all Buddhists try and develop the right kind of motivation—compassion, forgiveness and tolerance. I meditate six or seven times a day.

From nine until lunch I read and study our scriptures. Buddhism is a very profound religion and, although I have been studying all my life, there is still so much to learn.

Unfortunately nearly all our ancient books and manuscripts have been destroyed by the Chinese. It's as though all the Gutenberg bibles and Domesday books in the world had been destroyed. No record. No memory. Before the Chinese invasion, we had over six thousand functioning monasteries and temples. Now there are only thirty-seven.

I also try and read Western masters. I want to learn more about Western philosophy and science. Especially nuclear physics, astronomy and neurobiology. Often Western scientists come and discuss the relationship between our philosophy and theirs, or compare their work on the brain function and Buddhist experience of different levels of consciousness. It is an absorbing exchange, for all of us!

I often get up and go and fiddle with things. Charge batteries for the radio, repair something. From childhood I have been fascinated with mechanical things—toys, small cars, aeroplanes—things I could explore with my hands. We had an old movie projector in Lhasa that belonged to the Thirteenth Dalai Lama. It was looked after by an ancient Chinese monk. But when he died, no one else knew how to make it work. So I learnt how to make it go, but it was trial and error, as I couldn't read the instructions. I only spoke Tibetan. So now sometimes I work in my workshop repairing things like watches or clocks. Or planting things in the greenhouse. I love plants, especially delphiniums and tulips, and love to see them grow.

At twelve-thirty I have lunch, usually non-vegetarian, though I prefer vegetarian. I eat what I'm given. Sometimes thupka— soup with noodles, occasionally momo—steamed dumplings with meat—and skabakleb—deep-fried bread with meat inside.

The afternoon is taken up with official meetings with the *Bka'zhag* (Tibetan cabinet in exile), or deputies from the Assembly of Tibetan People's Deputies. But there are always people who come from Tibet, with or without the permission of the Chinese. Mostly without—brave people who escape over 17,000-foot Himalayan passes.

It is very painful for me. They all have sad stories and cry. Practically everyone tells me the names of relatives who have been killed by the Chinese, or died in Chinese prisons or labor camps. I try to give them encouragement and see how I can help them practically, as they arrive here destitute and in very bad health.

Very often they bring their children here. They tell me it is the only way they can learn our language, faith and culture. We put the younger ones in the Tibetan Children's Village here or in Mussoorie. Older ones who want to be monks we send for training in our monasteries in South India.

Although Tibetans want me to return, I get messages from *inside* not to return under the present circumstances. They don't want me to be a Chinese puppet like the Panchen Lama. Here, in the free world, I am more useful to my people as a spokesman. I can serve them better from outside.

Sometimes Pema, my youngest sister, who runs the Tibetan Children's Village for orphans here, comes and discusses problems. Like all monks, I don't see much of my family;

my parents are dead. My elder brother, Norbu, is Professor of Tibetan studies in Bloomington, Indiana. Thondup, a businessman, lives in Hong Kong.

Unfortunately my middle brother, Lobsang Samden, died two years ago. We were very close. He lived and studied with me in the Potala where we used to get up to all sorts of mischief. Before his death, he worked here at the medical center. I miss him very much.

At six I have tea. As a monk, I have no dinner. At seven it is television time, but unfortunately they transmit discussion programs. And as one is from Amritsar and the other from Pakistan, and I don't know Punjabi or Urdu, it's all talk to me. But occasionally there is a film in English. I liked the BBC series on western civilization, and those wonderful nature programs.

Then it's time for bed and more meditation and prayers and by eight-thirty or nine I fall asleep. But if there is a moon, I think that it is also looking down on my people imprisoned in Tibet. I give thanks that, even though I am a refugee, I am free here, free to speak for my people. I pray especially to the patron deity of Tibet, Avalokitesvara, for them. There is not one waking hour when I don't think of the plight of my people, locked away in their mountain fastness.

"Whether one believes in a religion or not, and whether one believes in rebirth or not, there isn't anyone who doesn't appreciate kindness and compassion."

—The Dalai Lama

5 Kindness and Compassion

I want to speak to you this evening about the importance of kindness and compassion. When I speak about this, I regard myself not as a Buddhist, not as the Dalai Lama, not as a Tibetan, but rather as one human being. And, I hope that you in the audience will, at this moment, think of yourselves as humans beings rather than as Americans, or Westerners, or members of any particular group. These things are secondary. If from my side and from the listeners' side we interact as human beings, we can reach this basic level. If I say, "I am a monk," or "I am a Buddhist," these are, in comparison to my nature as a human being, temporary. To be a human is basic. Once you are born as a human being, that cannot change until death. Other things—whether you are educated or uneducated, rich or poor—are secondary.

Today we face many problems. Some are created essentially by ourselves based on divisions due to ideology, religion, race, economic status, or other factors. Therefore, the time has come for us to think on a deeper level, on the human level, and from that level we should appreciate and respect the sameness of others as human beings. We must build closer relationships of mutual trust, understanding, respect, and help, irrespective of differences of culture, philosophy, religion, or faith.

After all, all human beings are the same—made of human flesh, bones, and blood. We all want happiness and want to avoid suffering. Further, we all have an equal right to be happy. In other words, it is important to realize our sameness as human beings. We all belong to one human family. That we quarrel with each other is due to secondary reasons, and all of this arguing with each other, cheating each other, suppressing each other is of no use.

Unfortunately, for many centuries, human beings have used all sorts of methods to suppress and hurt one another. Many terrible things have been done. It has meant more problems, more suffering, and more mistrust, resulting in more feelings of hatred and more divisions.

Today the world is becoming smaller and smaller. Economically, and from many other viewpoints, the different areas of the world are becoming closer and inceasingly interdependent. Because of this, international summit meetings often take place; problems in one remote place are connected with global crises. This situation expresses the fact that it is time, it is necessary, to think more on a human level rather than on the basis of the matters that divide us. Therefore, I am speaking to you as just a human being, and I earnestly hope that you also are listening with the thought, "I am a human being, and I am here listening to another human being."

All of us want happiness. In cities, on farms, even in remote places, people are busy and active. What is the main purpose of this activity? Everyone is trying to create happiness. To do so is right. However, it is very important to follow a correct method in seeking happiness. We must keep in mind that too much involvement on a superficial level will not solve the larger problems.

There are all about us many crises, many fears. Through highly developed science and technology, we have reached an advanced level of material progress that is both useful and necessary. Yet, if you compare the external progress with our internal progress, it is quite clear that our internal progress is inadequate. In many countries, crises—murders, wars and terrorism—are chronic. People complain about the decline in morality and the rise in criminal activity. Although in external matters we are highly developed and continue to progress, at the same time it is equally important to develop and progress in terms of inner development.

In ancient times, if there was war, the effect—the extent of destruction—was limited. Today, however, because of external material progress, the potential for destruction is beyond imagination. Last year I visited Hiroshima. Though I knew something about the nuclear explosion there, it was a very different matter physically to visit the place, to see it with my own eyes, and to meet with people who actually suffered at that moment. I was deeply moved. A terrible weapon was used. Though we might regard someone as an enemy, on a deeper level an enemy is also a human being, also wants happiness, and has the right to be happy. Looking at Hiroshima and thinking about this, at that moment I became even more convinced that anger and hatred cannot solve problems.

Anger cannot be overcome by anger. If a person shows anger to you, and you respond with anger, the result is disastrous. In contrast, if you control anger and show opposite attitudes—compassion, tolerance, and patience—then not only do you yourself remain in peace, but the other's anger will gradually diminish.

World problems similarly cannot be challenged by anger or hatred. They must be faced with compassion, love, and true kindness. Look at all the terrible weapons there are. Yet, the weapons themselves cannot start a war. The button to trigger them is under a human finger, which moves by thought, not under its own power. The responsibility rests in our thought.

If you look deeply into such things, the blueprint is found within—in the mind—out of which actions come. Thus, first controlling the mind is very important. I am not talking here about controlling the mind in the sense of deep meditation, but just about cultivating less anger, more respect for others' rights, more concern for other people, more clear realization of our sameness as human beings. Take the Western view of the Eastern bloc—for instance, of the Soviet Union. You must look at the Soviet Union as brothers and sisters; the people of Russia are the same as yourselves. The Russians also should look on this side as brothers and sisters. This attitude may not solve problems immediately, but we have to make the attempt. We have to begin promoting this understanding through magazines and through television. Rather than just advertising to make money for ourselves, we need to use these media for something meaningful, something seriously directed towards the welfare of humankind. Not money alone. Money is necessary, but the actual purpose of money is for human beings. Sometimes we lose interest in the human and are just concerned about money. This is not sensible.

After all, we all want happiness, and no one will disagree with the fact that with anger, peace is impossible. With kindness and love, peace of mind can be achieved. No one wants anger, no one wants mental unrest, yet because of ignorance, they occur. Bad attitudes, such as depression, arise from the power of ignorance, not of their own accord.

Through anger we lose one of the best human qualities— the power of judgement. We have a good brain, which other mammals do not have, allowing us to judge what is right and what is wrong, not only in terms of today's concerns, but considering ten, twenty, or even a hundred years in the future. Without any precognition, we can use our normal common sense to determine if something is a right or wrong method; we can decide that if we do such and such, it will lead to such and such an effect. However, once our mind is occupied by anger, we lose this power of judgement, and once lost, it is very sad. Physically you are a human being, but mentally you are incomplete. Given that we have this physical human form, we must safeguard our mental capacity for judgement. For that, we cannot take out insurance; the insurance company is within: self-discipline, self-awareness, and a clear realization of the disadvantages of anger and the positive effects of kindness. Thinking about this again and again, we can become convinced of it, and then with self-awareness, we can control the mind.

For instance, at present you may be a person who gets quickly and easily irritated by small things. With clear understanding and awareness, this can be controlled. If you usually remain angry for ten minutes, try to reduce it to eight. Next week make it five minutes and the next month two. Then make it zero. That is how to develop and train our minds.

This is my feeling and also the sort of practice I myself do. It is quite clear that everyone needs peace of mind. The question, then, is how to achieve it. Through anger we cannot; through kindness, through love, through compassion, we can achieve one individual's peace of mind. The result of this is a peaceful family—happiness between parents and children, fewer quarrels between husband and wife; no worry about divorce. Extended to the national level, this attitude can bring unity, harmony, and cooperation with genuine motivation. On the international level, we need mutual trust, mutual respect, frank and friendly discussion with sincere motivation, and joint effort to solve world problems. All these are possible.

But first we must change within ourselves. Our national leaders try their best to solve our problems, but when one problem is solved, another one crops up; trying to solve that, again there is another somewhere else. The time has come to try a different approach. Of course, it is very difficult to achieve such a worldwide movement for peace of mind, but it is the only alternative. If there were another method that was easier and more practical, it would be better, but there is none. If through weapons we could achieve real lasting peace, all right. Let all factories be turned into weapon factories. Spend every dollar for that—if we achieve definite lasting peace. But this is impossible.

Weapons do not remain stockpiled. Once a weapon is developed, sooner or later someone will use it. Someone might feel that if you do not use it, then millions of dollars are wasted, so somehow you should use it—drop a bomb to try it out. The result is that innocent people get killed.

Therefore, although it is difficult to attempt to bring about peace through internal transformation, this is the only way to achieve lasting world peace. Even if during my own lifetime it is not achieved, it is all right. More human beings will come, the next generation and the one after that, and progress can continue. I feel that despite the practical difficulties and the sense that this is regarded as an unrealistic view, it is worthwhile to make the attempt. Therefore, wherever I go, I express these things. I am encouraged that people from different walks of life generally receive it well.

Each of us has responsibility for all humankind. It is time for us to think of other people as true brothers and sisters and to be concerned with their welfare, with lessening their suffering. Even if you cannot sacrifice your own benefit entirely, you should not forget the concerns of others. We should think more about the future and benefit of all humanity.

Also, if you try to subdue your selfish motives—anger, and so forth—and develop more kindness and compassion for others, ultimately you yourself will benefit more than you would otherwise. So sometimes I say that the wise selfish person should practice this way. Foolish selfish people are always thinking of themselves, and the result is negative. Wise selfish people think of others, help others as much as they can, and the result is that they too receive benefit.

This is my simple religion. There is no need for temples; no need for complicated philosophy. Our own brain, our own heart is our temple; the philosophy is kindness.

6 Cooperation Among World Religions

One time in a monastery in Spain, near Barcelona, I met a Christian monk who spent five years in a hermitage behind the monastery. When I visited there he came to see me. His English was not good, in fact it was worse than mine. We couldn't talk much. We looked at each other's face. I got a very happy experience, some kind of vibration. This helped me to understand the real result of Christian practice. Christianity has a different method, tradition, philosophy. . .yet it produces such a person. I asked him: "What did you practice during your years in solitude?" "I concentrated on love," he told me. So you see, it is the same, isn't it? But this does not mean that all theories are identical. I feel a greater variety of theories may be more useful since there is a variety of people.

———————

Question: Why do different traditions vary so much in their explanation of truth and how to obtain it?

DL: For me Buddhist spiritual development is very useful as a guide for this life. But this does not mean that everyone should follow Buddhism. There are so many different mental dispositions. For certain people Buddhism simply cannot work. The different religions meet the needs of different people.

[From a talk given by the Dalai Lama at an ecumenical gathering in the United States—1979.]

That we have here a common gathering of various religious believers is a positive sign. Among spiritual faiths, there are many different philosophies, some just opposite to each other on certain points. Buddhists do not accept a creator; Christians base their philosophy on that theory. There are great differences, but I deeply respect your faith, not just for political reasons or to be polite, but sincerely. For many centuries your tradition has given great service to humankind.

When we pray together, I feel something, I do not know the exact words—whether you would call it blessings, or grace—but in any case there is a certain feeling that we can experience. If we utilize it properly, that feeling is very helpful for inner strength. For a real sense of brotherhood and sisterhood that feeling—that atmosphere and experience—is very useful and helpful. Therefore I particularly appreciate these ecumenical gatherings.

All of the different religious faiths, despite their philosophical differences, have a similar objective. Every religion emphasizes human improvement, love, respect for others, sharing other peoples' suffering. On these lines every religion has more or less the same viewpoint and the same goal. Those faiths which emphasize Almighty God and faith in and love of God have as their purpose the fulfillment of God's intentions. Seeing us all as creations of and followers of one God, they teach that we should cherish and help each other. The very purpose of faithful belief in God is to accomplish His wishes, the essence of which is to cherish, respect, love, and give service to our fellow humans.

Since an essential purpose of other religions is similarly to promote such beneficial feelings and actions, I strongly feel that from this viewpoint a central purpose of all the different philosophical explanations is the same. Through the various religious systems, followers are assuming a salutary attitude toward their fellow humans—our brothers and sisters—and implementing this good motivation in the service of human society. This has been demonstrated by a great many believers in Christianity throughout history; many have sacrificed their lives for the benefit of humankind. This is true implementation of compassion. When we Tibetans were passing through a difficult period, Christian communities from all over the world took it upon themselves to share our suffering and rushed to our help. Without regard for racial, cultural, religious, or philosophical differences, they regarded us as fellow humans and came to help. This gave us real inspiration and recognition of the value of love.

Although in every religion there is an emphasis on compassion and love, from the viewpoint of philosophy, of course there are differences, and that is all right. Philosophical teachings are not the end, not the aim, not what you serve. The aim is to help and benefit others, and philosophical teachings to support those ideas are valuable. If we go into the differences in philosophy and argue with and criticize each other, it is useless. There will be endless argument; the result will mainly be that we irritate each other—accomplishing nothing. Better to look at the purpose of the philosophies and to see what is shared—an emphasis on love, compassion, and respect for a higher force.

No religion basically believes that material progress alone is sufficient for humankind. All religions believe in forces beyond material progress. All agree that it is very important and worthwhile to make a strong effort to serve human society.

To do this, it is important that we understand each other. In the past, due to narrow-mindedness and other factors, there has sometimes been discord between religious groups. This should not happen again. If we look deeply into the value of a religion in the context of the worldwide situation, we can easily transcend these unfortunate happenings. For, there are many areas of common ground on which we can have harmony. Let us just be side by side—helping, respecting, and understanding each other—in a common effort to serve humankind. The aim of human society must be the compassionate betterment of human beings.

Question: As a religious leader, are you interested in actively encouraging others to join your faith? Or do you take the position of being available if someone should seek knowledge of your faith?

DL: This is an important question. I am interested not in converting other people to Buddhism but in how we Buddhists can contribute to human society, according to our own ideas. I believe that other religious faiths also think in a similar way, seeking to contribute to the common aim.

Because the different religions have at times argued with each other rather than concentrating on how to contribute to a common aim, for the last twenty years in India I have taken every occasion to meet with Christian monks—Catholic and Prostestant—as well as Muslims and Jews and, of course, in India, many Hindus. We meet, pray together, meditate together, and discuss their philosophical ideas, their way of approach, their techniques. I take great interest in Christian practices, what we can learn and copy from their system. Similarly, in Buddhist theory there may be points such as meditative techniques which can be practiced in the Christian church.

Just as Buddha showed an example of contentment, tolerance, and serving others without selfish motivation, so did Jesus Christ. Almost all of the great teachers lived a saintly life—not luxuriously like kings or emperors but as simple human beings. Their inner strength was tremendous, limitless, but the external appearance was of contentment with a simple way of life.

Question: Can there be a synthesis of Buddhism, Judaism, Christianity, Hinduism, and all religions, gathering the best in all, and forming a world religion?

DL: Forming a new world religion is difficult and not particularly desirable. However, in that love is essential to all religions, one could speak of the universal religion of love. As for the techniques and methods for developing love as well as for achieving salvation or permanent liberation, there are many differences between religions. Thus, I do not think we could make one philosophy or one religion.

Furthermore, I think that differences in faith are useful. There is a richness in the fact that there are so many different presentations of the way. Given that there are so many different types of people with various predispositions and inclinations, this is helpful.

At the same time, the motivation of all religious practice is similar—love, sincerity, honesty. The way of life of practically all religious persons is contentment. The teachings of tolerance, love, and compassion are the same. A basic goal is the benefit of humankind—each type of system seeking in its own unique ways to improve human beings. If we put too much emphasis on our own philosophy, religion, or theory, are too attached to it, and try to impose it on other people, it makes trouble. Basically all the great teachers, such as Gautama Buddha, Jesus Christ, or Mohammed, founded their new teachings with a motivation of helping their fellow humans. They did not mean to gain anything for themselves nor to create more trouble or unrest in the world.

Most important is that we respect each other and learn from each other those things that will enrich our own practice. Even if all the systems are separate, since they each have the same goal, the study of each other is helpful.

Question: Sometimes when we hear Eastern religions compared with Western culture, the West is made to seem materialistic and less enlightened than the East. Do you see such a difference?

DL: There are two kinds of food—food for mental hunger and food for physical hunger. Thus a combination of these two—

material progress and spiritual development is the most practical thing. I think that many Americans, particularly young Americans, realize that material progress alone is not the full answer for human life. Right now all of the Eastern nations are trying to copy Western technology. We Easterners such as Tibetans, like myself, look to Western technology feeling that once we develop material progress, our people can reach some sort of permanent happiness. But when I come to Europe or North America, I see that underneath the beautiful surface there is still unhappiness, mental unrest, and restlessness. This shows that material progress alone is not the full answer for human beings.

Washington, NJ., September 25, 1989
"The Dalai Lama taught us a lot about Buddhism, even more about menschlichkeit, and most of all about Judaism. As all true dialogue accomplishes, this encounter with the Dalai Lama opened us to the other faith's integrity. Equally valuable, the encounter reminded us of neglected aspects of ourselves, of elements in Judaism that are overlooked until they are reflected back to us in the mirror of the Other."
—Rabbi Irving Greenberg

"The Nazis came to my people as the Chinese to yours."
—Rabbi Laurence Kushner

An unusual Buddhist-Jewish dialogue took place today, at a Buddhist monastery situated on an idyllic green hill rising above the shopping malls and discount outlets of New Jersey.

"I want to learn the Jewish 'secret technique' of survival," said the Dalai Lama, who initiated the meeting. The spiritual and temporal leader of six million Tibetans as well as many thousands of Westerners said he was intrigued by several possible parallels between Judaism and Tibetan Buddhism. These included a devotion to scholarship and, in particular, a belief in the sacredness and interdependence of all life.

A *shofar* (ram's horn) and a *tallit* (prayer shawl) were given to the beaming Buddhist leader, who tucked the horn into his belt and slung the shawl over his monk's robes.

The lively discussion lasted for three hours, and though it centered on serious issues of maintaining cultural identity in spite of a diaspora, and comparisons of religious, cosmological and theological issues, it was punctuated with laughter.

On leaving the meeting, Rabbi Kushner spoke of the similarities between Tibetan Buddhism and the spiritual core of Judaism. "The core of Judaism is the irrepressible hunch that the unity of all beings is beyond all physical representation. This seems to be the essence of Buddhism," he said. "And the Buddhists' movement from that to love, compassion and non-violence is exactly what I always thought Judaism was—and still is."

7 Reason, Science and Spiritual Values

The Buddha says in a sutra:

> Monks and scholars should
> Well analyze my words,
> Like gold [to be tested through] melting, cutting
> and polishing,
> And then adopt them, but not for the sake of
> showing me respect.

These words of the Buddha mean that even if a particular doctrine is set forth in Buddha's scriptures, one must examine to determine whether or not it is damaged by reasoning. If there is damage by way of reasoning, it is not suitable to assert the literal reading of the passage.

———

Suppose that something is definitely proved through scientific investigation. That a certain hypothesis is verified or that a certain fact emerges as a result of scientific investigation. And suppose, furthermore, that that fact is incompatible with Buddhist theory. There is no doubt that we must accept the result of scientific research. You see, the general Buddhist position is that we must always accept fact. Mere speculation devoid of an empirical basis, when such is possible, will not do. So if an hypothesis has been tested, and has been found to be one hundred percent sure, then that is what we must accept.

I think this notion is at the very core of Buddhist thinking. It is the general Buddhist attitude. Buddhists believe in rebirth. But suppose that through various investigative means, science one day comes to the definite conclusion that there is no rebirth. If this is definitively proven, then we must accept it and we will accept it. This is the general Buddhist idea. So it seems that the scientific method is more powerful! But of course we know that there is a limit to this method also.

Basically a Buddhist attitude on any subject must be one that accords with the facts. If, upon investigation, you find that there is reason and proof for a point, then you should accept it. That is not to say that there are not certain points that are beyond the human powers of deductive reasoning—that is a different matter. But things such as the size or position of the moon and stars are things that the human mind can come to know. On these matters it is important to accept the facts, the real situation, whatever that may be.

When we investigate certain descriptions as they exist in our own texts, we find that they do not correspond to reality. In such a case we must accept the reality, and not the literal scriptural explanation. This should be the basic attitude.

What is the reason for presenting topics in such great detail? The root of suffering comes through the force of ignorance, and the destruction of ignorance is to be brought about by analytical wisdom. I will give a brief outline of the system of the Buddhist logic. In terms of the way in which analytical wisdom researches or investigates its objects, there are six modes of research or investigation, done with the purpose of eventually eradicating suffering. The first is to research the meaning of words, that is, to investigate word by word their meaning. The second is to research the actualities of things in terms of whether they are internal or external. The third is to research the character of phenomena—their individual, particular character and their general character. The fourth is to research the classes of phenomena in terms of where favorable and unfavorable qualities lie. The fifth is to research time, because the transformation of phenomena depends upon time. The sixth is to research reasoning, within which there are four types:

1   the reasoning of dependence: that effects depend upon causes
2   the reasoning of the performance of function: for example, that fire performs the function of burning or that water performs the function of moistening
3   the reasoning of nature: that each phenomenon has its own nature; for example, that fire has a nature of heat and water has a nature of wetness
4   the reasoning of valid establishment: non-contradiction with direct perception and inference

Valid cognition is of two types, direct and inferential valid cognition, the latter having three forms—inference by the power of the fact, inference through renown, and scriptural inference by way of believability.

The basis for generating an inferential consciousness is a logical sign. The importance of logical signs or reasons is due to the fact that an inferential consciousness is a figuring out of an object—usually hidden to direct perception—in dependence on a correct, unmistaken sign. The teachers of logic— Dignaga, Dharmakirti, and so forth—made presentations of the types of reasons in very detailed ways.

A correct sign, or reason, is tri-modal. In brief, this means that (1) the sign is established as being a property of the subject, (2) the forward pervasion is established, and (3) the counter-pervasion is established. Such correct signs are presented from many different viewpoints. In terms of their entity, correct signs are of three types—signs that are effects [from the presence of which the existence of their causes can be inferred], signs of the sameness of nature [as in the case of proving that something is a tree because of being an oak], and signs of non-observation [as in the case of proving the absence of something through its not being perceived despite fulfillment of the conditions for its perception if it were present].

In another way, when correct signs are divided in terms of the predicate being proven, there are two types—signs of a positive phenomenon and signs of a negative phenomenon. Then, in terms of the party to whom the proof is directed, there are correct signs on the occasion of one's own purpose—proving something to yourself through reasons—and correct signs on the occasion of another's purpose—proving something to another. Then, in terms of the mode of proof, there are five:

1   signs proving conventions—that is to say, you already know the meaning but need to know the name
2   signs proving meanings
3   signs proving mere conventions
4   signs proving mere meanings
5   signs proving both meanings and conventions.

All of these are included in signs that are effects, signs of the sameness of nature, and signs of non-observation, the first mode of division by way of entity. Relative to the specific time, situation, and person for whom one is stating a reason, one states an effect-sign, nature-sign, or non-observation sign.

Each of these three divisions by way of entity also has many subdivisions. For instance, effect signs are of five types: those proving (1) an actual cause, (2) a preceding cause, (3) a general cause, (4) a particular cause, and (5) a correct effect sign which is a means of inferring causal attributes. Similarly, among signs of non-observation, there are correct non-observation signs of the non-appearing and correct signs which are non-observations of what is suitable to appear if it were present. These are further subdivided into eleven types, some scholars even making twenty-five, such as non-observation of a related object, non-observation of a cause, or observation of a contradictory object.

Among the six modes of investigation, the last is the research of reasoning which, as mentioned above, is divided into four types. It seems that scientific investigation is mostly by way of three of these—the reasoning of nature, in which the basic character of an object is researched; the reasoning of the performance of function, in which the functions that an object performs based on having a certain nature are researched; the reasoning of dependence, in which that on which the object depends is researched. These seem to be the basic modes of procedure of science. Therefore, it seems that the six types of investigation cover all of both scientific and spiritual research. I believe that scientific research and development should work together with meditative research and development since both are concerned with similar objects. The one proceeds through experiment by instruments, and the other, through inner experience and meditation. A clear distinction should be made between what is not found by science and what is found to be non-existent by science. What science finds to be non-existent, a Buddhist necessarily must accept as non-existent, but what science merely does not find is a completely different matter. It is quite clear that there are many, many mysterious things. The human senses reach a certain level, but we cannot say that there is nothing beyond what we perceive with our five senses. Even what our own grandparents did not perceive with their five senses, we are finding nowadays with ours. Thus, even within physical phenomena with shape and color, etc., those things that we can see with our five senses, many that we do not understand now, will be understood in the future.

With respect to other fields such as consciousness itself, though sentient beings, including humans, have experienced consciousness for centuries, we still do not know what consciousness actually is—its functioning, its complete nature. Such things that have no form, no shape, and no color are in a category of phenomena that cannot be understood in the way that external phenomena are investigated.

The Buddhist view of consciousness is very complex and

detailed. The basic Buddhist definition of consciousness is that which is clear and knowing. In order to promote a variety of insights and realizations with respect to consciousness, it is divided from many different points of view.

It does seem as though modern physics accepts some sort of elementary partless particle. One begins with a physical form that can be seen by the eye and analyzes it, subdividing it further and further experimentally. One finally is said to reach a substantial entity which can no longer be subdivided, and that is said to be partless. As long as it can be further subdivided, it is said to have parts, and when one reaches the limits of divisibility, that entity is said to be partless.

The Buddhist notion of partlessness, or its refutation, is not something that is actually based on experimentation. The Buddhist discussion of this subject does not deal with the empirical divisions of matter into different parts. It is instead a theoretical treatment of the possibility of spatial or dimensional partlessness that we set forth. In regards to consciousness it is not spatial partlessness that is discussed (since consciousness is non-material and hence non-spatial) but temporal partlessness. So, in discussions of partlessness, the "parts" being referred to in the Buddhist context are not empirically tested distinct subdivisions. Instead, material things are divided into spatial parts and consciousness is divided into temporal parts, in a strictly theoretical and abstract way.

Question: Please give examples of phenomena that science does not find.

DL: Consciousness itself. Every moment we have many different levels of consciousness—coarse and subtle. Never mind the subtler levels of consciousness, it is difficult to identify even the coarser levels.

Question: If mind is more than brain or a physical phenomenon, why can thinking be altered and controlled through taking drugs or through stimulation of the brain?

DL: There are many different kinds of consciousness or mind. Certain ones are very much related to the physical level. For example, our present eye consciousness is dependent upon the physical eye organ; therefore, if something has happened in the organ, the consciousness cannot function normally, and if the eye organ is removed, the consciousness cannot remain, barring an organ transplant.

In any case, certain consciousnesses are very much related with present organs and brain cells; these consciousnesses can be controlled through surgery on the brain or through electronic methods. However, the subtler levels of mind are more independent of the body; thus these consciousnesses are more difficult to affect through physical means.

Question: Do you think that we in the West must learn to bring the paths of spiritual and scientific investigation together in order to prevent harm to humankind?

DL: If we only concentrate on scientific development, without concerning ourselves with spiritual development—if we lose a sense of human value—it will be dangerous. After all, the aim of scientific progress itself is to benefit humankind. If scientific development goes wrong and brings more suffering and more tragedy on humankind, this is unfortunate. I believe that mental development and material development must go side by side.

In this century, when human intelligence has been so enriched by the new knowledge derived through important scientific discoveries, fortunately a new trend is emerging. People in the scientific disciplines are taking a fresh interest in spiritual and moral concepts and are prepared to reappraise their attitudes towards the relevance of spiritual development in order to achieve a more complete view of life and the world. In particular, there is a growing interest among the scientific community in Buddhist philosophical thought. I am optimistic that over the next few decades there will be a great change in our world view both from the material and the spiritual perspectives.

Question: Buddhism has so much knowledge and understanding about the mind but in the West we have so little. Do you think the mind will be the next area for Western scientists to explore?

DL: I believe that Western science will develop towards a more synthetic view of its different branches...psychology, biology and physics. It will find a connecting link, a relation between these areas of experience. In the past the scientific and the spiritual or mental development have been regarded as separate from each other, as two different paths leading in opposite directions. But now, in the late twentieth century, this view is beginning to change.

Newport Beach, CA, October 8, 1989
"Presentations by the cognitive scientists...were distinguished by the extremely close attention paid by His Holiness and by the acuity of his scientific intuition. Time and again he would anticipate the flow of logic or experiment."
—Professor Newcomb Greenleaf

To those who have observed the Dalai Lama over the years, his intensive participation in conferences with neuroscientists comes as no surprise. The winner of the 1989 Nobel Peace Prize has long demonstrated a deep interest in things scientific—and particularly in the interface between science and Buddhism.

Recently he attended a Mind and Life conference in Newport Beach, California, with psychiatrists from Harvard Medical School and prominent neuroscientists including Lewis L. Judd, director of the National Institute of Mental Health. Topics ranged from amnesia and memory to lucid dreaming. Although the presentations were made by the Westerners, the scientists made it clear that they regarded the conference as an opportunity to learn from the Tibetans. "Here's an ancient system with an extremely refined insight on the mind that may have something to tell us," commented Larry R. Squire of the University of California, San Diego.

Two years ago a first Mind and Life conference was held in Dharamsala, the Himalayan seat of the Tibetan government in exile. There a group of scientists spent an intensive week with the Tibetan leader, discussing issues in cognitive science—from artificial intelligence to molecular biochemistry.

That he was awarded the Peace Prize is a tribute to the Dalai Lama's ability to serve as a bridge between various factions. In his conferences with neuroscientists, this great world leader has shown that he acts not only as a bridge between various viewpoints, but as a synthesizer of them as well.

8 Meditation

Would you like to participate in an experiment in meditation? First, look to your posture: arrange the legs in the most comfortable position; set the backbone as straight as an arrow. Place your hands in the position of meditative equipoise, four finger widths below the navel, with the left hand on the bottom, right hand on top, and your thumbs touching to form a triangle. This placement of the hands has connection with the place inside the body where inner heat is generated. Bending the neck down slightly, allow the mouth and teeth to be as usual, with the top of the tongue touching the roof of the mouth near the top teeth. Let the eyes gaze downwards loosely—it is not necessary that they be directed to the end of the nose; they can be pointed toward the floor in front of you if this seems more natural. Do not open the eyes too wide nor forcefully close them; leave them open a little. Sometimes they will close of their own accord; that is all right. Even if your eyes are open, when your mental consciousness becomes steady upon its object, these appearances to the eye consciousness will not disturb you.

For those of you who wear eye glasses, have you noticed that when you take off your glasses, because of the unclarity there is less danger from the generation of excitement and more danger of laxity? Do you find that there is a difference between facing and not facing the wall? When you face the wall, you may find that there is less danger of excitement or scattering. These kinds of things can be determined through your own experience.

Within meditations that have an object of observation, there can be two types of objects: external or internal. Now, instead of meditating on the mind itself, let us meditate on an external object of observation—for instance, the body of a Buddha for those who like to look at a Buddha or a cross for those who like that, or whatever symbol is suitable for you. Mentally visualize that the object is about four feet in front of you, at the same height as the eyebrows. The object should be approximately two inches high and emanating light. Try to conceive of it as being heavy, for this will prevent excitement. Its brilliance will prevent laxity. As you concentrate, you must strive for two factors: first, to make the object of observation clear, and second, to make it steady.

Has something appeared to your mind? Are the sense objects in front of your eyes bothering you? If that is the case, it is all right to close them, but with the eyes closed, do you see a reddish appearance? If you see red with the eyes closed or if you are bothered by what you see when your eyes are open, you are too involved with the eye consciousness and thus should try to withdraw attention from the eye consciousness and put it with the mental consciousness.

That which interferes with the steadiness of the object of observation and causes it to fluctuate is excitement or, in a more general way, scattering. To stop that, withdraw your mind more strongly inside so that the intensity of the mode of apprehension begins to lower. To withdraw the mind, it helps to think about something that makes you more sober, a little bit sad. These thoughts can cause your heightened mode of apprehension of the object, the mind's being too tight, to lower or loosen somewhat whereby you are better able to stay on the object of observation.

It is not sufficient just to have stability. It is necessary also to have clarity. That which prevents clarity is laxity, and what causes laxity is an over-withdrawal, excessive declination, of the mind. First of all, the mind becomes lax; this can lead to lethargy in which, losing the object of observation, you have as if fallen into darkness. This can lead even to sleep. When this occurs, it is necessary to raise or heighten the mode of apprehension. As a technique for that, think of something that you like, something that makes you joyous, or go to a high place or where there is a vast view. This technique causes the deflated mind to heighten in its mode of apprehension.

It is necessary within your own experience to recognize when the mode of apprehension has become too excited or too lax and determine the best practice for lowering or heightening it.

The object of observation that you are visualizing has to be held with mindfulness. Then, along with this, you inspect, as if from a corner, to see whether the object is clear and stable; the faculty that engages in this inspection is called introspection. When powerful steady mindfulness is achieved, introspection is generated, but the uncommon function of introspection is to inspect from time to time to see whether the mind has come under the influence of excitement or laxity. When you develop mindfulness and introspection well, you are able to catch laxity and excitement just before they arise and prevent their arising.

Briefly, that is how to sustain meditation with an external object of observation.

Another type of meditation involves looking at the mind itself. Try to leave your mind vividly in a natural state, without thinking of what happened in the past or of what you are planning for the future, without generating any conceptuality. Where does it seem that your consciousness is? Is it with the eyes or where is it? Most likely you have a sense that it is associated with the eyes since we derive most of our awareness of the world through vision. This is due to having relied too much on our sense consciousnesses. However, the existence of a separate mental consciousness can be ascertained; for example, when attention is diverted by sound, that which appears to the eye consciousness is not noticed. This indicates that a separate mental consciousness is paying more attention to sound heard by the ear consciousness than to the perceptions of the eye consciousness.

With persistent practice, consciousness may eventually be perceived or felt as an entity of mere luminosity and knowing, to which anything is capable of appearing and which, when appropriate conditions arise, can be generated in the image of whatsoever object. As long as the mind does not encounter the external circumstance of conceptuality, it will abide empty without anything appearing in it, like clear water. Its very entity is that of mere experience. Let the mind flow of its own accord without conceptual overlay. Let the mind rest in its natural state, and observe it. In the beginning, when you are not used to this practice, it is quite difficult, but in time the mind appears like clear water. Then, stay with this unfabricated mind without allowing conceptions to be generated. In realizing this nature of the mind, we have for the first time located the object of observation of this internal type of meditation.

The best time for practicing this form of meditation is in the morning, in a quiet place, when the mind is very clear and alert. It helps not to have eaten too much the night before nor to sleep too much; this makes the mind lighter and sharper the next morning. Gradually the mind will become more and more stable; mindfulness and memory will become clearer.

See if this practice makes your mind more alert throughout the day. As a temporary benefit your thoughts will be tranquil. As your memory improves, gradually you can develop a kind of special perception and understanding, which is due to an increase of mindfulness. As a long term benefit, because your mind has become more alert and sharp, you can utilize it in whatever field you want.

If you are able to do a little meditation daily, withdrawing this scattered mind on one object inside, it is very helpful. The conceptuality that runs on thinking of good things, bad things, and so forth and so on will get a rest. It provides a little vacation just to set a bit in non-conceptuality and have a rest.

There is yet another method of meditation which enables one to discern the ultimate nature of phenomena. This type of meditation involves analytical introspection. Generally, phenomena are divided into two types: the mental and physical aggregates—or phenomena that are used by the I—and the I that uses them. To determine the nature of this I, let us use an example. When we say John is coming, there is some person who is the one designated by the name John. Is this name designated to his body? It is not. Is it designated to his mind? If it were designated to his mind, we could not speak of John's mind. Mind and body are things used by the person. It almost seems that there is an I separate from mind and body. For instance, when we think, "Oh, my lousy body!" or "My lousy mind!", to our own innate mode of appearance the mind itself is not the I, right? Now, what John is there who is not his mind or body? You also should apply this to yourself, to your own sense of I—where is this I in terms of mind and body?

When my body is sick, though my body is not I, due to the body's being sick it can be posited that I am sick. In fact, for the sake of the well-being and pleasure of the I, it sometimes even becomes necessary to cut off part of the body. Although the body is not the I, there is a relationship between the two: the pain of the body can serve as the pain of the I. Similarly, when the eye consciousness sees something, it appears to the mind that the I perceives it.

What is the nature of the I? How does it appear to you? When you do not fabricate or create any artificial concept in your mind, does it seem that your I has an identity separate from your mind and body? But if you search for it, can you find it? For instance, someone accuses you, "You stole this," or "You ruined such and such," and you feel, "I didn't do that." At that time, how does the I appear? Does it appear as if solid? Does some solid, steady, and strong thing appear to your mind when you think or say, "I didn't do that?"

This seemingly solid, concrete, independent, self-instituting I under its own power that appears at such a time actually does not exist at all, and this specific non-existence is what is meant by selflessness. In the absence of analysis and investigation, a mere I as in, "I want such and such," or "I am going to do such and such," is asserted as valid, but the non-existence of an independent or self-powered I constitutes the selflessness of the person. This selflessness is what is found when one searches analytically to try to find the I.

Such non-inherent existence of the I is an ultimate truth, a final truth. The I that appears to a non-analytical conventional awareness is the dependently arisen I that serves as the basis of the conventions of action, agent, and so forth; it is a conventional truth. In analyzing the mode of subsistence or the status of the I, it is clear that although it appears to exist inherently, it does not, much like an illusion.

That is how the ultimate nature of the I—emptiness—is analyzed. Just as the I has this nature, so all other phenomena that are used by the I are empty of inherent existence. When analyzed, they cannot be found at all, but without analysis and investigation, they do exist. Their nature is the same as the I.

The conventional existence of the I as well as of pleasure and pain make it necessary to generate compassion and altruism, and because the ultimate nature of all phenomena is this emptiness of inherent existence, it is also necessary to cultivate wisdom. When these two aspects—compassion and wisdom—are practiced in union, wisdom grows more profound, and the sense of duality diminishes. Due to the mind's dwelling in the meaning of emptiness, dualistic appearance becomes lighter, and at the same time the mind itself becomes more subtle. As the mind grows even more subtle, reaching the subtlest level, it is eventually transformed into the most basic mind, the fundamental innate mind of clear light, which at once realizes and is of one taste with emptiness in meditative equipoise without any dualistic appearance at all, mixed with emptiness. Within all having this one taste, anything and everything can appear; this is known as "All in one taste, one taste in all."

These are a few of the types of meditation practiced in the Tibetan tradition. Of course there are many other techniques such as mantra an so forth. Perhaps now we could have some discussion.

Question: Why is it better to meditate in the morning?

DL: There are two main reasons. Physically, in the early morning—once you are used to it—all the nerve centers are fresh, and this is beneficial. Also, there is a difference just in terms of the time. Further, if you have slept well, you are more fresh and alert in the morning; this we can see in our own experience. At night I reach a point where I cannot think properly; however, after sleeping and the waking in the early morning, that thing, which yesterday I could not properly think through, automatically appears more clearly. This shows that mental power is much sharper in the morning.

Question: What is the most expedient means for overcoming resistance to meditation?

DL: Five faults are explained as obstacles to meditation. The first is laziness; second is to forget the advice on the object, that is, to forget the object; next are laxity and excitement; then failure to apply an antidote when laxity or excitement are present, and the last is to continue applying the antidotes when laxity or excitement have already been overcome. These are called the five faults. Eight antidotes are explained for them. The antidotes to laziness are, first of all, the faith that intelligently sees the value of meditative stabilization, the prime value being that without it the higher paths cannot be generated. In dependence upon ascertaining the good qualities of meditative stabilization, the aspiration which seeks to attain those qualities is induced. By means of that, exertion comes whereby you eventually attain pliancy causing body and mind to be free from unfavorable states and to be serviceable in a virtuous direction such that whatever virtue is done is powerful. These four are the antidotes to the first fault, laziness.

It is helpful not to practice too long in the beginning; do not over-extend yourself; the maximum period is around fifteen minutes. The important thing is not the length of the session but the quality of it. If you meditate too long, you can become sleepy, and then your meditation will become a matter of becoming accustomed to that state. This is not only a waste of time but also a habit that is difficult to eliminate in the future. In the beginning, start with many short sessions—even eight or sixteen sessions in a day—and then as you get used to the processes of meditation, the quality will improve, and the session will naturally become longer.

A sign that your meditative stabilization is progressing well is that even though your meditative session may be long, it will feel as though only a short time has passed. If it seems that you have spent a long time in meditation even though you have spent only a little, this is a sign that you should shorten the length of the session. This can be very important at the beginning.

Question: Could you say something more about effort? Isn't a great deal of effort necessary?

DL: Effort is crucial in the beginning for generating a strong will. We all have the Buddha nature and thus already have within us the substances through which, when we meet with the proper conditions, we can turn into a fully enlightened being having all beneficial attributes and devoid of all faults. The very root of failure in our lives is to think, "Oh, how useless and powerless I am!" It is important to have a strong force of mind thinking, "I can do it," this not being mixed with pride or any other afflictive emotion.

Moderate effort over a long period of time is important, no matter what you are trying to do. One brings failure on oneself by working extremely hard at the beginning, attempting to do too much and then giving it all up after a short time. A constant stream of moderate effort is needed. Similarly, when meditating, you need to be skillful by having frequent, short sessions; it is more important that the session be good quality than it be long.

When you have such effort, you have the necessary "substances" for developing concentration. Concentration is a matter channelizing this mind which is presently distracted in a great many directions. A scattered mind does not have much power. When channelized, no matter what the object of observation is, the mind is very powerful.

There is no external way to channelize the mind, as by a surgical operation; it must be done by withdrawing it inside. Withdrawal of the mind also occurs in deep sleep in which the factor of alertness has become unclear; therefore, here the withdrawal of the mind is to be accompanied by very strong clarity of alertness. In brief, the mind must have stability staying firmly on its object, great clarity of the object, and alert, clear, sharp tautness.

Question: What is the relationship of the mind and afflictive emotions?

DL: The very entity of the mind, its nature of mere luminosity and knowing, is not polluted by defilements; they do not abide in the entity of the mind. Even when we generate afflictive emotions, the very entity or nature of the mind is still mere luminosity and knowing, and because of this we are able to remove the afflictive emotions. If you agitate the water in a pond, it becomes cloudy with mud; yet the very nature of the water itself is not dirty. When you allow it to become still again, the mud will settle, leaving the water pure.

How are the defilements removed? They are not removed

by outside action nor by leaving them as they are; they are removed by the power of antidotes, meditative antidotes. To understand this, take the example of anger. All anger is impelled and polluted by improper conceptuality.

Both the object of our anger and subject, oneself, appear to exist concretely, as if established by way of their own character. Both seem forcefully to exist in their own right. But as I was saying earlier, things do not actually exist in this concrete way. As much as we are able to see an absence of independent self-existence, that much will our conception of over-reification and its assistance to anger be lessened.

The sign that our perceptions are superimposing a goodness or badness beyond what is actually present is that while desirous or angry we feel that the object is terrifically good or bad but afterwards when we think about the experience, it is laughable that we viewed the object that way; we understand that our perception was not true. These afflicted states do not have any valid support. The mind which analytically searches for the independent self-existence of an object finds ascertainment of its lack of independent self-nature through valid reasoning, and thus this kind of understanding does have a valid foundation. Like a debate in court, one perception is based on reason and truth, while the other one is not. When the evidence is sufficient, in such a debate the true view eventually overpowers the other because it can withstand analysis.

It is impossible for the mind simultaneously to apprehend one object in contradictory ways. With respect to one object, therefore, as you get used to understanding its non-inherent nature, not only is it impossible at that time to generate a conception of inherent nature but also as strong as the correct realization becomes, so much, in general, does conception of its opposite weaken in force.

To generate such wisdom we engage in meditation because our minds, as they are now, are not very powerful. Our mind is presently scattered; its energies need to be channeled like the way water in a hydroelectric plant is channeled to create great force. We achieve this with the mind through meditation, channeling it such that it becomes very forceful, at which point it can be utilized in the direction of wisdom. Since all the substances for enlightenment exist within ourselves, we should not look for Buddhahood somewhere else.

Question: Does emptiness also mean fullness?

DL: It seems so. Usually, I explain that emptiness is like a zero. A zero itself is nothing, but without a zero you cannot count anything; therefore, a zero is something, yet zero.

Question: Would you please say something about the nature of *mandalas.*

DL: Mandala, in general, means that which extracts the essence. There are many usages of the term *mandala* according to context. One type of mandala is the offering of the entire world system, with the major and minor continents mentally constructed, to high beings. Also, there are painted mandalas, mandalas of concentration, those made out of colored sand, mandalas of the conventional mind of enlightenment, mandalas of the ultimate mind of enlightenment, and so forth. Because one can extract a meaning from each of these through practicing them, they are all called mandalas.

Although we might call these pictures and constructed depictions mandalas, the main meaning is for oneself to enter into the mandala and extract an essence in the sense of receiving blessing. It is a place of gaining magnificence. Because one is gaining a blessing and thereupon developing realizations it is called an extraction or assumption of something essential.

Question: How does one choose a teacher of spiritual subjects or know a teacher to be reliable?

DL: This should be done in accordance with your interest and disposition, but you should analyze well. You must investigate before accepting a lama or teacher to see whether that person is really qualified or not. It is said in a scripture that just as fish that are hidden under the water can be seen through the movement of the ripples from above, so also a teacher's inner qualities can, over time, be seen a little through that person's behavior.

We need to look into the person's scholarship—the ability to explain topics—and whether the person implements those teachings in his or her conduct and experience.

9 A Talk to Western Buddhists

We are gathered here today generally speaking because each of us is seeking a deeper meaning in life. In the past few days I have said many times that along with material progress, inner development is important and useful. You yourselves can observe that when persons who have inner strength face problems, they are better equipped to confront them. In the case of Tibet and my own experience, limited though it may be, I have found this to be true. Someone in my position, in a complicated situation and having large responsibilities may, under such circumstances, come to have some mental problems. However, as you may read from my face, I am not much bothered. Of course, we realize the very great problems, the tragedy; yet we accept them as facts and try our best. There is no doubt that an attitude of inner strength can help; it influences the way we approach and confront problems.

Since everyone has more or less the same nature, the practice of religion, in this case Buddhism, has something deep and useful for one's life. This is not necessarily to bring good rebirth, and so forth; even within this one life if we adopt a right attitude toward our fellow humans, that itself will give in return great satisfaction. The principles are good motivation and compassion.

Although compassion is explained mainly in the *Bodhisattva* scriptures—the Great Vehicle (*Mahayana*)—all Buddhist ideas are based on compassion. All of Buddha's teachings can be expressed in two sentences. The first is, "You must help others." This includes all the Great Vehicle teachings. "If not, you should not harm others." This is the whole teaching of the Low Vehicle (*Hinayana*), or *Theravadayana*. It expresses the basis of all ethics, which is to cease harming others. Both teachings are based on the thought of love, compassion. A Buddhist should, if possible, help others. If this is not possible, at least do not do any harm to others.

When we practice, initally, as a basis we control ourselves, stopping the bad actions which hurt others as much as we can. This is defensive. After that, when we develop certain qualifications, then as an active goal we should help others. In the first stage, sometimes we need isolation while pursuing our own inner development; however, after you have some confidence, some strength, you must remain with, contact, and serve society in any field—health, education, politics, or whatever.

There are people who call themselves religious-minded, trying to show this by dressing in a peculiar manner, maintaining a peculiar way of life, and isolating themselves from the rest of society. That is wrong. A scripture of mind-purification (mind-training) says, "Transform your inner viewpoint, but leave your external appearance as it is." This is important. Because the very purpose of practicing the Great Vehicle is service for others, you should not isolate yourselves from society. In order to serve, in order to help, you must remain in society.

That is one point. The second is that particularly in Buddhism while we practice we must use the brain as well as the heart. On the ethical side, we must practice the quality of a good and warm heart; also, since Buddhism is very much involved in reasoning and logic—the wisdom side—intelligence is important. Thus, a combination of mind and heart is needed. Without knowledge, without fully utilized intelligence, you cannot reach the depths of the Buddhist doctrine; it is very difficult to achieve concrete or fully qualified wisdom. There may be exceptions, but this is the general rule.

It is necessary to have a combination of hearing, thinking, and meditating. When engaging in hearing, it is important to mix the mind, to familiarize the mind, with what is being heard. The study of religion is not like learning about history. It must be mixed with your mental continuum; your mind should be suffused with it. A *sutra* says that the practices are like a mirror; your actions of body, speech, and mind are like a face to be seen in the mirror; and through the practices you should recognize faults and gradually get rid of them. As it is said in the oral transmission, "If there is enough space between yourself and the practices for someone else to walk through, then you are not implementing them properly." In that case, the practices become something like an object of entertainment. And if it is that, it can turn into an object of argument. Then after a good deal of argument, it can even lead to fighting. This is not at all the purpose of religion.

While we are learning the practices, we must relate them to our own behavior. There is a story of a *Gadamba* scholar-yogi who was reading in the Discipline (*Vinaya*) that it was not suitable to use an animal skin on one's seat; he was sitting on a bearskin, so he immediately pulled it out from under himself. Then as he read further, he learned that it was permissible to use such if the weather was cold or the person was sick, and so he carefully brought it back. This is true practice—immediately to implement what one is learning.

If one is learning religion in general or Buddhism as an academic study, it is different right from the beginning. The motivation is just to acquire knowledge of another topic of learning. However, we who are supposed to be Buddhists, who are supposed to practice, should try to implement the teachings while we are learning. Then we can experience their real value.

The third point I would like to make is that when you start practicing, you should not expect too much. We live in a time of computers and automation, so you may feel that inner development is also an automatic thing for which you press a button and everything changes. It is not so. Inner development is not easy and will take time. External progress, the latest space missions and so forth, have not reached their present level within a short period but over centuries, each generation making greater developments based on those of the previous generation. However, inner development is even more difficult since internal improvement cannot be transferred from generation to generation. Your past life's experience very much influences this life, and this life's experience becomes the basis for the next rebirth's development, but transference of inner development from one person to another is impossible. Thus, everything depends on yourself, and it will take time.

I have met Westerners who at the beginning were very enthusiastic about their practice, but after a few years have completely forgotten it, and there are no traces of what they had practiced at one time. This is because at the beginning they expected too much. Shantideva's *Engaging in the Bodhisattva Deeds* emphasizes the importance of the practice of patience—tolerance. This tolerance is an attitude not only towards your enemy but also an attitude of sacrifice, of determination, so that you do not fall into the laziness of discouragement. You should practice patience, or tolerance, with great resolve. This is important.

Let me use myself as an example. I was born into a Buddhist family in a country which is primarily Buddhist, although there are also Christians and Muslims as well as many followers of the ancient Tibetan religion, Bon. I was able to learn Buddhism in my native language and from a very young age became a monk. Thus, from the viewpoint of practicing the Buddhist doctrine, I had much more facility than you. But in terms of my own development, around fifteen or sixteen years of age I began to have real enthusiasm for practice. I have been practicing since then and now am forty-four. Looking back over those years, I can notice there has been improvement over periods of two to three years. Within a few weeks, I can notice very little. Thus determination to practice without loosening effort is very important.

Inner development comes step by step. You may think, "Today my inner calmness, my mental peace, is very small," but still, if you compare, if you look five, ten, or fifteen years back, and think "What was my way of thinking then? How much inner peace did I have then and what is it today?"—comparing it with what it was then, you can realize that there is some progress, there is some value. This is how you should compare—not with today's feeling and yesterday's feeling, or last week or last month, even not last year, but five years ago. Then you can realize what improvement has occurred internally. Progress comes by maintaining constant effort in daily practice.

People sometimes ask me whether Buddhism—an ancient teaching which comes from the East—is suitable for Westerners or not. My answer is that the essence of all religions deals with basic human problems. As long as human beings, either Western or Eastern—white, black, yellow, or red—have the sufferings of birth, disease, old age, and death, all are equal in that respect. As long as these basic human sufferings are there, since the essential teaching is concerned with that suffering, there is not much question whether it is suitable or not.

Still, there is a question with regard to each individual's mental disposition. For some individuals a certain religion brings more benefit whereas in other cases another brings more benefit. Under the circumstances, the variety of teachings found in human society is necessary and useful, and among Westerners, no doubt there are people who find Buddhism suitable to their requirements.

When we speak of the essence, there is no question about suitability and no need to change the basic doctrines. However, on the superficial level change is possible. A Burmese monk in the Theravada tradition whom I met recently in Europe and for whom I developed great respect makes the distinction between cultural heritage and religion itself. I call this a distinction between the essence of a religion and the superficial ceremonial or ritual level. In India, Tibet, China, Japan, or wherever, the religious aspect of Buddhism is the same, but the cultural heritage is different in each country. Thus, in India, Buddhism incorporated Indian culture; in Tibet, Tibetan culture, and so on. From this viewpoint, the incorporation of Western culture into Buddhism may also be possible.

The essence of the Buddhist teachings does not change; wherever it goes it is suitable; however, the superficial aspects—certain rituals and ceremonies—are not necessarily suitable for a new environment; those things will change. How they will change in a particular place we cannot say. This evolves over time. When Buddhism first came from India to Tibet, no one had the authority to say, "Now Buddhism has come to a new land; from now on we must practice it in this way or that way." There was no such decision. It gradually evolved, and in time a unique tradition arose. Such may be the case for Westerners; gradually, in time, there may be a Buddhism combined with Western culture. In any case, this generation—your generation—who are starting this new idea in new countries have a big responsibility to take the essence and adjust it to your own environment.

For this we must use the brain to investigate. You should not go to either extreme—too conservative is not good, too radical is also not good. As in our Middle Way theory, one should follow a middle course. It is very important to keep a middle approach in every field. Even in our daily consumption of food, we must follow a moderate way. With too much in our stomachs, trouble will come to us; too little is not sufficient. So, in our daily life—in our whole way of life -it is important to remain in the middle; both extremes must be checked. This brain must have full knowledge about the environment and the cultural heritage—full knowledge about what sort of things are of value in day to day life and what things, though part of the cultural heritage, may not be useful in daily life.

In the case of Tibetan culture, for example, certain past traditions may not be useful in the future. When under new circumstances the social system and way of social thinking change, certain aspects of a culture may no longer be useful. In the same way, if in the United States and Canada there are some aspects of the old culture which are not useful in modern daily life, they should be modified, and other aspects which are still meaningful and useful should be retained. You should try to combine that culture and Buddhism.

If you really take an interest in Buddhism, then the most important thing is implementation—practice. To study Buddhism and then use it as a weapon in order to criticize others' theories or ideologies is wrong. The very purpose of religion is to control yourself, not to criticize others. Rather, we must criticize ourselves. How much am I doing about my anger? About my attachment, about my hatred, about my pride, my jealousy? These are the things which we must check in daily life with the knowledge of Buddhist teachings. Clear?

As Buddhists, while we practice our own teaching, we must respect other faiths, Christianity, Judaism, and so forth. We must recognize and appreciate their contributions over many past centuries to human society, and at this time we must strive to make common effort to serve humankind. The adopting of a right attitude toward other faiths is particularly important for new Buddhists to keep in mind.

Also among Buddhists, there are different schools, different systems of practice, and we should not feel that one teaching is better, another teaching is worse, and so on. Sectarian feeling and criticism of other teachings or other sects is very bad, poisonous, and should be avoided.

The most important thing is practice in daily life; then you can know gradually the true value of religion. Doctrine is not meant for mere knowledge but for the improvement of our minds. In order to do that, it must be part of our life. If you put religious doctrine in a building and when you leave the building depart from the practices, you cannot gain its value.

I hope that you engage in practice with a good heart and from that motivation contribute something good to Western society. That is my prayer and wish.

———

Question: What is the role of the teacher in practice? Is it necessary to have a teacher?

DL: Yes, but it depends on the subject. General subjects, general Buddhist ideas, can be learned through books without a teacher. But certain complicated subjects are difficult to understand by just reading books without an experienced person's instruction and explanation.

Question: A person, particularly in the West, must have the foundation of humility, honesty and an ethical way of life. Once one has this foundation, what else does Your Holiness suggest that one cultivate in one's life, if there is the foundation of virtue, ethics and humility?

DL: The next thing to be cultivated is mental stabilization. Ethics is a method to control oneself—it is a defensive action. Our actual enemy, you see, is within ourselves. The afflicted emotions (pride, anger, jealousy) are our real enemies. These are the real trouble makers, and they are to be found within ourselves. The actual practice of religion consists of fighting against these inner enemies.

As in any war, first we must have a defensive action, and in our spiritual fight against the negative emotions, ethics is our defense. Knowing that at first one is not fully prepared for offensive action, we first resort to defensive action and that means ethics. But once one has prepared one's defenses, and has become somewhat accustomed to ethics, then one must launch one's offensive. Here our main weapon is wisdom. This weapon of wisdom is like a bullet, or maybe even a rocket, and the rocket launcher is mental stabilization or calm abiding. In brief, once you have a basis in morality or ethics, the next step is to train in mental stabilization and eventually in wisdom.

Question: Could you please give us some brief advice which we can take with us into our daily lives?

DL: I don't know, I don't really have that much to say. I'll simply say this. We are all human beings, and from this point of view we are the same. We all want happiness and we do not want suffering. If we consider this point, we will find that there are no differences between people of different faiths, races, color or cultures. We all have this common wish for happiness.

Actually, we Buddhists are supposed to save all sentient beings, but practically speaking, this may be too broad a notion for most people. In any case, we must at least think in terms of helping all human beings. This is very important. Even if we cannot think in terms of sentient beings inhabiting different worlds, we should nonetheless think in terms of the human beings on this planet. To do this is to take a practical approach to the problem. It is necessary to help others, not only in our prayers, but in our daily lives. If we find we cannot help others, the least we can do is to desist from harming them. We must not cheat others or lie to them. We must be honest human beings, sincere human beings.

On a very practical level, such attitudes are things which we need. Whether one is a religious believer, a religious person, or not, is another matter. Simply as an inhabitant of the world, as a member of the human family, we need this kind of attitude. It is through such an attitude that real lasting world peace and harmony can be achieved. Through harmony, friendship, and respecting one another, we can solve many problems. Through such means, it is possible to overcome problems in the right way, without difficulties.

This is what I believe, and wherever I go, whether it be to a communist country like the Soviet Union or Mongolia, or to a capitalist and democratic country like the United States and the countries of Western Europe, I express this same message. This is my advice, my suggestion. It is what I feel. I myself practice this as much as I can. If you find you agree with me, and you find some value in what I have said, then it has been worthwhile.

You see, sometimes religious persons, people who are genuinely engaged in the practice of religion, withdraw from the sphere of human activity. In my opinion, this is not good. It is not right. But I should qualify this. In certain cases, when a person genuinely wishes to engage in intensive meditation, then it is alright to seek isolation for certain limited periods of time. But such cases are by far the exception, and the vast majority of us must work out a genuine religious practice within the context of human society.

In Buddhism, both learning and practice are extremely important and they must go hand in hand. Without knowledge, just to rely on faith, faith and more faith is good but not sufficient. So the intellectual part must definitely be present. At the same time, strictly intellectual development without faith and practice, is also of no use. It is necessary to combine knowledge born from study with sincere practice in our daily lives. These two must go together.

Question: Your Holiness has spoken of service. How can we be of service in Western society?

DL: If you help even only one person, that is help. There is great opportunity to help others in the field of education, in schools, colleges, and so forth. Many Christian brothers and sisters are carrying out such work which I admire very much and from which Buddhists must learn. So in the fields of education and health, you can give direct service.

Also in jobs such as working for a company or as a factory worker, even though you may not be directly helping others, indirectly you are serving society. Even though you are doing it for the sake of your salary, indirectly it does help people, and you should do it with a good motivation, trying to think, "My work is meant to help people." If you were making guns or bullets, of course it would be difficult. If you are making bullets and all the time thinking, "I am doing this to help others," it would be hypocritical, wouldn't it?

Question: I do not feel worthwhile as a person. How can I work on this as a beginning meditation student?

DL: You should not be discouraged. Human potential is the same for all. Your feeling, "I am of no value," is wrong. Absolutely wrong. You are deceiving yourself. We all have the power of thought—so what are you lacking? If you have will power, then you can do anything. If you become discouraged, thinking, "How could such a person as me possibly do anything?", then there is no way you can succeed. Therefore, in Buddhism it is usually said that you are your own master. You can do anything.

Question: Can one attain enlightenment without separating from the world?

DL: Certainly. To renounce the world means to give up your attachment to the world. It does not mean that you have to separate yourself from it. The very purpose of the Buddhist doctrine is to serve others. In order to serve others you must remain in the society. You should not isolate yourself from the rest of society.

Question: Accomplishing all that is required on the path (study, intruction, meditation) and working to provide food, shelter and protection for one's family are two full time commitments. How can we balance all of our commitments?

DL: One has to do as much of both of these as one can. This is my own position, for I myself try to do certain practices but at the same time carry out work that essentially benefits others. For people whose circumstances are similar to mine, the most important aspect is to cultivate a good motivation and to carry out your daily program within it. Early in the morning as well as late in the night, you can spend at least half an hour in practice—meditation, recitation, daily yoga, or the like. Then, while working during the day, you should remember the motivation.

Each morning before working, you should establish a determination to carry out today's work in accordance with the teaching and for the maximum usefulness to other beings. In the evening, before going to bed, check what you have done during the day, whether or not you actually acted in accordance with that initial determination. That is how to perform daily practice.

10 *Living Sanely*

Right from the moment of our birth, we are under the care and kindness of our parents, and then later on in our life when we are oppressed by sickness and become old, we are again dependent on the kindness of others. Since at the beginning and end of our lives we are so dependent on others' kindness, how can it be in the middle that we would neglect kindness towards others?

———

Love and kindness are the very basis of society. If we lose these feelings, society will face tremendous difficulties; the survival of humanity will be endangered.

———

Together with material development, we need spiritual development so that inner peace and social harmony can be experienced. Without inner peace, without inner calm, it is difficult to have lasting external peace.

———

Question: You often speak about the need for mental peace. What do you mean by it? Does it denote a specific state of mind?

DL: Mental peace? If you reduce anger and attachment, you reach a point when your mind always remains calm or stable. It is as simple as that. Strong anger and attachment create waves in your mind. People may not realize when they yield to desire or develop attachment that it will cause them mental unrest. But actually, when a strong desire or attachment occurs, during that moment mental peace is lost. To reduce attachment, especially anger or hatred, leads to mental calmness. This is what we call mental peace.

Question: Isn't it also necessary to practice meditation to obtain mental peace?

DL: My experience is that it is obtained mainly through reasoning. Meditation does not help much.

The main cure is to realize how harmful, how negative, anger is. Once you realize very clearly, very convincingly how negative it is, that realization itself has power to reduce anger. You must see that it always brings unhappiness and trouble.

Of course anger comes. Anger is like a friend or relative which you cannot avoid and always have to associate with. When you get to know him you realize that he is difficult and that you have to be careful. Every time you meet that person— still on friendly terms—you take some precaution. As a result the influence that he has over you grows less and less. In the same way you see the anger coming, but you realize "Ah, it always brings trouble, there is not much point to it." The anger will lose its power or force. So with time it gets weaker and weaker.

———

Question: To watch your mind, isn't that meditation too?

DL: If you meditate like that during the meditation period you may find mental peace, or some kind of realization, but that may simply be a diversion from the real problem. The problem is still there. The approach by way of reasoning is not a diversion. You meet anger, negativity and so forth, and because of your mental preparedness the influence of the anger is lessened.

———

When you pass through a difficult period, you can react by losing your determination or hope and getting depressed. That of course is very sad, very negative. But the difficult situation can also open your eyes to the real situation, the truth. Look at human history. Human history is in a way the history of human mental thought. Historical events, wars, good developments, tragedies. . .all these are records of negative and positive human thought. All the great persons, the liberators, the great thinkers, all these great human beings of the past, have been produced through positive thought. Tragedy, tyranny, all the terrible wars, all those negative things have happened because of negative human thought. In the human mind both positive and negative thoughts are potentially present. Therefore the only worthwhile thing for a human being to do is to try to develop the positive thought, to increase its power or force and to reduce the negative thinking. If you do that, human love, forgiveness, kindness will give you more hope and determination. And hope and determination will bring you a brighter future. If you give way to anger, hatred, you get lost. No sensible human being wants to lose himself or herself.

This is not a spiritual teaching, not a moral injunction. It is a fact that can be verified by today's experience. So in order to develop human determination you need hope. And to develop hope you need compassion, love. Love and compassion are the basis of hope and determination. So every spiritual teaching of the world emphasizes the importance of love and kindness.

Now, another point is that human happiness, human satisfaction ultimately must come from within oneself. It is wrong to expect some final satisfaction to come from money or from a computer.

Question: You have seen and experienced the kind of problems that people have in the West. Do you think that the main cause of those problems is neglect of the inner life?

DL: Yes.

Question: And will the cure to a large extent come through becoming more inwardly aware?

DL: Yes, there is no doubt about that.

Question: What is the main method to foster this inner awareness?

DL: Introspection and reasoning is more efficient for this purpose than meditation and prayer.

We can never obtain peace in the world if we neglect the inner world and don't make peace with ourselves. World peace must develop out of inner peace. Without inner peace it is impossible to achieve world peace, external peace. Weapons themselves do not act. They have not come out of the blue. Man has made them. But even given those weapons, those terrible weapons, they cannot act by themselves. As long as they are left alone in storage, they cannot do any harm. A human being must use them. Someone must push the button. Satan, the evil powers, cannot push that button. Human beings must do it.

When we contemplate death and the impermanence of life, our minds automatically begin to take an interest in spiritual achievements, just as an ordinary person becomes apprehensive upon seeing the corpse of a friend. Meditation on impermanence and death is very useful, for it cuts off attraction toward transient and meaningless activities.

Try to develop a deep conviction that the present human body has great potential and that you shall never waste even a single minute of its use. Not taking any essence of this precious human existence, but just wasting it, is almost like taking poison while being fully aware of the consequences of doing so. It is very wrong for people to feel deeply sad when they lose some money, while when they waste the precious moments of their lives they do not have the slightest feeling of repentance.

If you are mindful of death, it will not come as a surprise—you will not be anxious. You will feel that death is merely like changing your clothes. Consequently, at that point you will be able to maintain your calmness of mind.

To be aware of a single shortcoming within oneself is more useful than to be aware of a thousand in somebody else. Rather than speaking badly about people and in ways that will produce friction and unrest in their lives, we should practice a purer perception of them, and when we speak of others, speak of their good qualities. If you find yourself slandering anybody, just fill your mouth with excrement. That will break you of the habit quickly enough.

The negative emotions such as hatred, anger, and desire are our real enemies which disturb and destroy our mental happiness and cause disturbance in society. Therefore, they are totally to be abandoned; they do not have even the slightest potential for yielding happiness.

Often, when something appears to us as good, it appears to us as one hundred percent good, and when something appears to us as undesirable, it appears as though it were totally undesirable in its own right. As a result of such appearance we misapprehend the object, and then on this basis we misconceptualize its nature. At the moment that we have very strong anger towards an object, we experience the person toward whom we feel extremely angry as totally negative—right from the top of his crown to the end of his sole. When the force of the anger diminishes, then the person begins to appear to be a little better. A similar sequence of experience is true in the case of desire. When one is under a very strong influence of negative emotions, one is almost at the point of insanity. If we lose our mental balance, we will not be able to work for our own benefit, let alone work for others.

Tolerance can be learned only from an enemy; it cannot be learned from your spiritual teacher. At these lectures, for instance, you cannot learn tolerance, except perhaps when you are bored! You can only learn some of these positive spiritual qualities in the presence of enemies. Therefore, in a way, enemies are precious, in that they help us to grow.

If I had stayed in Lhasa and there had not been a Chinese invasion, I might still be isolated. I'd probably be more conservative than I am.

Therefore, I am very grateful to the Chinese for giving me this opportunity. The enemy is very important. The enemy teaches you inner strength. Your mind by nature is very soft, but when you have troubles, your mind gets strong.

If we were forced to choose between a sense of practical application and learnedness, a sense of practical application would be more important, for one who has this will receive the full benefit of whatever he knows. The mere learnedness of one whose mind is not tamed can produce and increase bad states of consciousness, which cause unpleasantness for himself and others instead of the happiness and peace of mind that were intended. One could become jealous of those higher than oneself, competitive with equals and proud and contemptuous towards those lower and so forth. It is as if medicine had be-

come poison. Because such danger is great, it is very important to have a composite of learnedness, a sense of practical
application and goodness, without having learnedness destroy
the sense of practical application or having the sense of practical application destroy learnedness.

————

Whenever I go someplace new, I think "New country, new
people," but ultimately, when I go deeper, all people are the
same. I feel very happy about this.

————

I prefer informality. Year by year, that conviction grows more
and more with me.

————

One of the most important things is compassion. We cannot
buy it in one of New York City's big shops. You cannot produce it by machine. But by inner development, yes.

————

How do we create peace and happiness? With weapons? Of
course not. With money? In some cases, but not all. But in
love, in sharing other people's suffering, yes. Good motivation is a sound basis for peace.

————

Question: How can one work with deep fears most effectively?

DL: There are quite a number of methods. The first is to think
about actions and their effects. Usually when something bad
happens, we say, "Oh, very unlucky," and when something
good happens, we say, "Oh, very lucky." Actually, these two
words, lucky and unlucky, are insufficient. There must be some
reason. Because of a reason, a certain time became lucky or
unlucky, but usually we do not go beyond lucky or unlucky.
The reason, according to the Buddhist explanation, is our past

karma, our actions.

One way to work with deep fears is to think that the fear comes as a result of your own actions in the past. Further, if you have fear of some pain or suffering, you should examine whether there is anything you can do about it. If you can, there is no need to worry about it; if you cannot do anything, then there is also no need to worry.

Another technique is to investigate who is becoming afraid. Examine the nature of your self. Where is this I? Who is I? What is the nature of I? Is there an I besides my physical body and my consciousness? This may help.

Also, someone who is engaging in the Bodhisattva practices seeks to take others' suffering onto himself or herself. When you have fear, you can think, "Others have fear similar to this; may I take to myself all of their fears." Even though you are opening yourself to greater suffering, taking greater suffering to yourself, your fear lessens.

Yet another way is not to let your mind stay with the thought of fear but to put it on something else and let the fear just become lost. That is just a temporary method. Also, if you have a sense of fear due to insecurity, you can imagine for instance, if you are lying down, that your head is in Buddha's lap. Sometimes this may help psychologically. Another method is to recite mantras.

Question: Please speak on the subject of love and marriage.

DL: I do not have much to say. My simple opinion is that making love is alright, but for marriage, don't hurry, be cautious. Make sure you will remain forever, at least for this whole life. That is important, for if you marry hurriedly without understanding well what you are doing, then after a month or after a year, trouble starts and you will be seeking divorce. From a legal viewpoint, divorce is possible, and without children it is maybe acceptable, but with children, it is not. It is not sufficient that a couple think of only their own love affairs and their own pleasure. You have a moral responsibility to think of your children. If the parents divorce, the child is going to suffer, not just temporarily, but for his or her whole life. The model for a person is one's own parents. If the parents are always fighting and finally divorce, I think that unconsciously, deep down, the child is badly influenced, imprinted. This is a tragedy. Thus, my advice is that for real marriage, there is no hurry: proceed very cautiously, and marry only after good understanding; then you will have a happy marriage. Happiness in the home will lead to happiness in the world.

His Holiness has become over the past 30 years a symbol of peace and a leading international spokesperson for the cause of non-violent social change. His spiritual and political leadership of Tibetans has been the principal force for the preservation of the Tibetan culture and way of life. His ongoing efforts to achieve a peaceful political resolution to the crisis in Tibet is our greatest hope for a future for Tibet that guarantees Tibetan human and political rights, and insures the survival of Tibetan culture.

As a member of the Congressional Human Rights Caucus, I am delighted that the Congressional Human Rights Foundation has chosen to present its 1989 Raoul Wallenberg Human Rights Award to the Dalai Lama. His Holiness' commitment to the principles of peace, human dignity, and human rights is an inspiration to us all, and there could be a no more fitting recipient of this honor.

—Congressman Mel Levine
Congressional Record, July 18, 1989

11 Human Rights and
Universal Responsibilities

At this time when our world is becoming smaller and more interdependent, when populations are growing rapidly and contacts among peoples and their governments are increasing, it is important to consider and reassess the position, rights and responsibilities of individuals, nations and peoples with respect to each other and to the planet as a whole.

The presence here in Strasbourg of so many persons, who are concerned about the rights and freedoms of their brothers and sisters in different and often far-away parts of the world, is an indication of the new closeness which is developing between us. It results from the growing recognition that the hopes of all human beings are essentially the same: we all seek happiness and try to avoid suffering, regardless of where we live and what our race, religion, sex or political situation may be.

I speak to you today as a fellow human being, an inhabitant of this planet which we are destined to share. I speak to you also as a simple Buddhist monk, a believer in the value and power of love and compassion, which are the essence of my own faith.

Human beings, indeed all sentient beings—human as well as animal—have a right to pursue happiness and live in peace. On the other hand, no one has the right to inflict pain and suffering on others.

Lack of understanding of the true nature of happiness, it seems to me, is the principal reason why people inflict sufferings on others. They think either that the other's pain may somehow be a cause of happiness for themselves or that their own happiness is more important, regardless of what pain it may cause. But this is shortsighted, no one truly benefits from causing harm to another sentient being. Whatever immediate advantage is gained at the expense of someone else is short-lived. In the long run causing others misery and infringing their rights to peace and happiness result in anxiety, fear and suspicion within one-self. Such feelings undermine the peace of mind and contentment which are the marks of happiness.

True happiness comes not from a limited concern for one's own well-being, or that of those one feels close to, but from developing love and compassion for all sentient beings. Here, love means wishing that all sentient beings should find happiness, and compassion means wishing that they should all be free of suffering. The development of this attitude gives rise to a sense of openness and trust that provides the basis for peace.

When we demand the rights and freedoms we so cherish, we should also be aware of our human responsibilities. If we accept that others have an equal right to peace and happiness as ourselves, have we not a responsibility to do what we can to help those in need and at least avoid harming them? Closing our eyes to our neighbor's suffering in order to better enjoy our own freedom and good fortune is a rejection of such responsibilities. We need to develop a concern for the problems of others, whether they be individuals or entire peoples.

In today's highly interdependent world, individuals and nations can no longer resolve many of their problems by themselves. We need one another. We must, therefore develop a sense of universal responsibility. This is the belief which I have been expressing ever since my first visit to Europe and the West in 1973. I am encouraged that an increasing number of people have come to share this view. There is a growing awareness of people's responsibilities to each other and to the planet we share. Even though so much suffering continues to be inflicted upon individuals and peoples in the name of ideology, religion, history or development, a new hope is emerging for the downtrodden. People everywhere are displaying a willingness to sacrifice their own well-being and, at times, their lives for the rights and freedoms of their fellow human beings. The recent success of struggles for human rights and democracy in a number of Asian countries and elsewhere could not have taken place without the sympathy, support and concern of people like yourselves who feel a responsibility to help others.

We are indeed witnessing a tremendous and popular movement for the advancement of human rights and democratic freedoms in the world. This movement has such moral force that even determined governments and armies are incapable of suppressing it. It is an encouraging indication of the triumph of the human spirit for freedom.

The growth of democratic freedoms of individuals as well as increasing recognition of the rights of nations and peoples—regardless of their political status—fills many of us with courage and hope for the future. It is natural and just for nations and peoples to demand respect for their rights and freedoms and to struggle to end repression, racism, military occupation and various forms of colonialism and alien domination. Governments should actively and consistently support such demands instead of only paying lip-service to general principles.

We are at the dawn of an age in which extreme political concepts and dogmas may cease to dominate human affairs. We must use this historic opportunity to replace them by universal human and spiritual values and ensure that these values become the fiber of the global family which is emerging.

It is our collective and individual responsibility to protect and nurture the global family, to support its weaker members and to preserve and tend to the environment in which we all live.

The Tibetan people wish to make their contribution and to fulfil their responsibilites. We are not a large and powerful people, but our way of life, our culture and spiritual tradition have helped us, even in the face of great hardship and suffering, to follow the path of peace and to find comfort in the pursuit of love and compassion.

Given the opportunity, the Tibetan people long to transform the high plateau, which is their home, into a true sanctuary of peace, where human beings and nature can live in harmony and peace.

We wish in our own modest way to promote the peace and human rights which all members of the global family seek.

12 An Ethical Approach To Environmental Protection

Peace and survival of life on earth as we know it are threatened by human activities that lack a commitment to humanitarian values. Destruction of nature and natural resources results from ignorance, greed and lack of respect for the earth's living things.

This lack of respect extends even to the earth's human descendants, the future generations who will inherit a vastly degraded planet if world peace does not become a reality, and if destruction of the natural environment continues at the present rate.

Our ancestors viewed the earth as rich and bountiful, which it is. Many people in the past also saw nature as inexhaustibly sustainable, which we know is the case only if we care for it.

It is not difficult to forgive destruction in the past which resulted from ignorance. Today, however, we have access to more information; it is essential that we re-examine ethically what we have inherited, what we are responsible for, and what we will pass on to coming generations.

Many of the earth's habitats, animals, plants, insects and even micro-organisms that we know to be rare may not be known at all by future generations. We have the capability and the responsibility to act; we must do so before it is too late.

Just as we should cultivate gentle and peaceful relations with our fellow human beings, we should also extend that same kind of attitude towards the natural environment. Morally speaking, we should be concerned for our whole environment.

This, however, is not just a question of morality or ethics, but a question of our own survival. For this generation and for future generations, the environment is very important. If we exploit the environment in extreme ways, we may receive some benefit today, but in the long run, we will suffer, as will our future generations. When the environment changes, the climatic condition also changes. When the climate changes dramatically, the economy and many other things change. Our physical health will be greatly affected. Again, conservation is not merely a question of morality, but a question of our own survival.

Therefore, in order to achieve more effective environmental protection and conservation, internal balance within the human being himself or herself is essential. The negligence of the environment, which has resulted in great harm to the human community, resulted from our ignorance of the very special importance of the environment. We must now help people to understand the need for environmental protection. We must teach people that conservation directly aids our survival.

If you must be selfish, then be wise and not narrow-minded in your selfishness. The key point lies in the sense of universal responsibility. That is the real source of strength, the real source of happiness. If we exploit everything available, such as trees, water and minerals, and if we don't plan for our next generation, for the future, then we're at fault, aren't we? However, if we have a genuine sense of universal responsibility as our central motivation, then our relations with the environment, and with all our neighbors, will be well balanced.

Ultimately, the decision to save the environment must come from the human heart. The key point is a call for a genuine sense of universal responsibility that is based on love, compassion and clear awareness.

13 The Nobel Evening Address
Oslo, Norway

Brothers and Sisters:

It is a great honor to come to this place and to share some of my thoughts with you. Although I have written a speech, it has already been circulated [see Chapter 1]. You know, some of my friends told me it is better to speak in Tibetan and have it translated into English; some say it is better to read my English statement; and some say it is better to speak directly with my broken English. I don't know. Yesterday, I tried my best to be formal but today I feel more free, so I will speak informally. In any case, the main points of my speech are on paper for you to see.

I think it advisable to summarize some of the points that I will consider. I usually discuss three main topics. Firstly, as a human being, as a citizen of the world, every human being has a responsibility for the planet. Secondly, as a Buddhist monk, I have a special connection with the spiritual world. I try to contribute something in that field. Thirdly, as a Tibetan I have a responsibility to the fate of the Tibetan nation. On behalf of these unfortunate people, I will speak briefly about their concerns.

So now, firstly, what is the purpose of life for a human being? I believe that happiness is the purpose of life. Whether or not there is a purpose to the existence of the universe or galaxies, I don't know. In any case, the fact is that we are here on this planet with other human beings. Then, since every human being wants happiness and does not want suffering, it is clear that this desire does not come from training, or from some ideology. It is something natural. Therefore, I consider that the attainment of happiness, peace, and joy is the purpose of life. Therefore, it is very important to investigate what are happiness and satisfaction and what are their causes.

I think that there is a mental factor as well as a physical factor. Both are very important. If we compare these two things, the mental factor is more important, superior to the physical factor. This we can know through our daily life. Since the mental factor is more important, we have to give serious thought to inner qualities.

Then, I believe compassion and love are necessary in order for us to obtain happiness or tranquility. These mental factors are key. I think they are the basic source. What is compassion? From the Buddhist viewpoint there are different varieties of compassion. The basic meaning of compassion is not just a feeling of closeness, or just a feeling of pity. Rather, I think that with genuine compassion we not only feel the pains and suffering of others but we also have a feeling of determination to overcome that suffering. One aspect of compassion is some kind of determination and responsibility. Therefore, compassion brings us tranquility and also inner strength. Inner strength is the ultimate source of success.

When we face some problem, a lot depends on the personal attitude towards that problem or tragedy. In some cases, when one faces the difficulty, one loses one's hope and becomes discouraged and then ends up depressed. On the other hand, if one has a certain mental attitude, then tragedy and suffering bring one more energy, more determination.

Usually, I tell our generation we are born during the darkest period in our long history. There is a big challenge. It is very unfortunate. But if there is a challenge then there is an opportunity to face it, an opportunity to demonstrate our will and our determination. So from that viewpoint I think that our generation is fortunate. These things depend on inner qualities, inner strength. Compassion is very gentle, very peaceful, and soft in nature, not harsh. You cannot destroy it easily as it is very powerful. Therefore, compassion is very important and useful.

Then, again, if we look at human nature, love and compassion are the foundation of human existence. According to some scientists, the foetus has feeling in the mother's womb and is affected by the mother's mental state. Then the few weeks after birth are crucial for the enlarging of the brain of the child. During that period, the mother's physical touch is the greatest factor for the healthy development of the brain. This shows that the physical needs some affection to develop properly.

When we are born, our first action is sucking milk from the mother. Of course, the child may not know about compassion and love, but the natural feeling is one of closeness toward the object that gives the milk. If the mother is angry or has ill feeling, the milk may not come fully. This shows that from our first day as human beings the effect of compassion is crucial.

If unpleasant things happen in our daily life, we immediately pay attention to them but do not notice other pleasant things. We experience these as normal or usual. This shows that compassion and affection are part of human nature.

Compassion or love has different levels; some are more mixed than others with desire or attachment. For example, parents' attitudes toward their children contain a mixture of desire and attachment with compassion. The love and compassion between husband and wife—especially at the beginning of marriage when they don't know the deep nature of each other—are on a superficial level. As soon as the attitude of one partner changes, the attitude of the other becomes opposite to what it was. That kind of love and compassion is more of the nature of attachment. Attachment means some kind of feeling of closeness projected by oneself. In reality, the other side may be very negative, but due to one's own mental attachment and projection, it appears as something nice. Furthermore, attachment causes one to exaggerate a small good quality and make it appear 100% beautiful or 100% positive. As soon as the mental attitudes change, that picture completely changes. Therefore, that kind of love and compassion is, rather, attachment.

Another kind of love and compassion is not based on something appearing beautiful or nice, but based on the fact that the other person, just like oneself, wants happiness and does not want suffering and indeed has every right to be happy and to overcome suffering. On such a basis, we feel a sense of responsibility, a sense of closeness toward that being. That is true compassion. This is because the compassion is based on reason, not just on emotional feeling. As a consequence, it does not matter what the other's attitude is, whether negative or positive. What matters is that it is a human being, a sentient being that has the experience of pain and pleasure. There is no reason not to feel compassion so long as it is a sentient being.

The kinds of compassion at the first level are mixed, interrelated. Some people have the view that some individuals have a very negative, cruel attitude towards others. These kinds of individuals appear to have no compassion in their minds. But I feel that these people do have the seed of compassion. The reason for this is that even these people very much appreciate it when someone else shows them affection. A capacity to appreciate other people's affection means that in their deep mind there is the seed of compassion.

Compassion and love are not man-made. Ideology is man-made, but these things are produced by nature. It is important to recognize natural qualities, especially when we face a problem and fail to find a solution. For example, I feel that the Chinese leaders face a problem which is in part due to their own ideology, their own system. But when they try to solve that problem through their own ideology, then they fail to tackle that problem. In religious business, sometimes even due to religion, we create a problem. If we try to solve that problem using religious methods, it is quite certain that we will not succeed. So I feel that when we face those kind of problems, it is important to return to our basic human quality. Then I think we will find that solutions come easier. Therefore, I usually say that the best way to solve human problems is with human understanding.

It is very important to recognize the basic nature of humanity and the value of human qualties. Whether one is educated or uneducated, rich or poor, or belongs to this nation or that nation, this religion or that religion, this ideology or that ideology, is secondary and doesn't matter. When we return to this basis, all people are the same. Then we can truly say the words *brother, sister*; then they are not just nice words—they have some meaning. That kind of motivation automatically builds the practice of kindness. This gives us inner strength.

What is my purpose in life, what is my responsibility? Whether I like it or not, I am on this planet, and it is far better to do something for humanity. So you see that compassion is the seed or basis. If we take care to foster compassion, we will see that it brings the other good human qualities. The topic of compassion is not at all religious business; it is very important to know that it is human business, that it is a question of human survival, that is not a question of human luxury. I might say that religion is a kind of luxury. If you have religion, that is good. But it is clear that even without religion we can manage. However, without these basic human qualities we cannot survive. It is a question of our own peace and mental stability.

Next, let us talk about the human being as a social animal. Even if we do not like other people, we have to live together. Natural law is such that even bees and other animals have to live together in cooperation. I am attracted to bees because I like honey—it is really delicious. Their product is something that we cannot produce, very beautiful, isn't it? I exploit them too much, I think. Even these insects have certain responsibilities, they work together very nicely. They have no constitution, they have no law, no police, nothing, but they work together effectively. This is because of nature. Similarly, each part of a flower is not arranged by humans but by nature. The force of nature is something remarkable. We human beings, we have constitutions, we have law, we have a police force, we have religion, we have many things. But in actual practice, I think that we are behind those small insects.

Sometimes civilization brings good progress, but we become too involved with this progress and neglect or forget about our basic nature. Every development in human society should take place on the basis of the foundation of the human nature. If we lose that basic foundation, there is no point in such developments taking place.

In cooperation, working together, the key thing is the sense of responsibility. But this cannot be developed by force as has been attempted in eastern Europe and in China. There a tremendous effort has to be made to develop in the mind of every individual human being a sense of responsibility, a concern for the common interest rather than the individual interest. They aim their education, their ideology, their efforts to brainwash, at this. But their means are abstract, and the sense of responsibility cannot develop. The genuine sense of responsibility will develop only through compassion and altruism.

The modern economy has no national boundaries. When we talk about ecology, the environment, when we are concerned about the ozone layer, one individual, one society, one country cannot solve these problems. We must work together. Humanity needs more genuine cooperation. The foundation for the development of good relations with one another is altruism, compassion, and forgiveness. For small arguments to remain limited, in the human circle the best method is forgiveness. Altruism and forgiveness are the basis for bringing humanity together. Then no conflict, no matter how serious, will go beyond the bounds of what is truly human.

I will tell you something. I love friends, I want more friends. I love smiles. That is a fact. How to develop smiles? There are a variety of smiles. Some smiles are sarcastic. Some smiles are artificial—diplomatic smiles. These smiles do not produce satisfaction, but rather fear or suspicion. But a genuine smile gives us hope, freshness. If we want a genuine smile, then first we must produce the basis for a smile to come. On every level of human life, compassion is the key thing.

Now, on the question of violence and non-violence. There are many different levels of violence and non-violence. On the basis of external action, it is difficult distinguish whether an action is violent or non-violent. Basically, it depends on the motivation behind the action. If the motivation is negative, even though the external appearance may be very smooth and gentle, in a deeper sense the action is very violent. On the contrary, harsh actions and words done with a sincere, positive motivation are essentially non-violent. In other words, violence is a destructive power. Non-violence is constructive.

When the days become longer and there is more sunshine, the grass becomes fresh and, consequently, we feel very happy. On the other hand, in autumn, one leaf falls down and another leaf falls down. These beautiful plants become as if dead and we do not feel very happy. Why? I think it is because deep down our human nature likes construction, and does not like destruction. Naturally, every action which is destructive is against human nature. Constructiveness is the human way. Therefore, I think that in terms of basic human feeling, violence is not good. Non-violence is the only way.

Practically speaking, through violence we may achieve something, but at the expense of someone else's welfare. That way, although we may solve one problem, we simultaneously seed a new problem. The best way to solve problems is through human understanding, mutual respect. On one side make some concessions; on the other side take serious consideration about the problem. There may not be complete satisfaction, but something happens. At least future danger is avoided. Non-violence is very safe.

Before my first visit to Europe in 1973, I had felt the importance of compassion, altruism. On many occasions I expressed the importance of the sense of universal responsibility. Sometimes during this period, some people felt that the

Dalai Lama's idea was a bit unrealistic. Unfortunately, in the Western world Gandhian non-violence is seen as passive resistance more suitable to the East. The Westerners are very active, demanding immediate results, even in the course of daily life. But today the actual situation teaches non-violence to people. The movement for freedom is non-violent. These recent events reconfirm to me that non-violence is much closer to human nature.

Again, if there are sound reasons or bases for the points you demand, then there is no need to use violence. On the other hand, when there is no sound reason that concessions should be made to you but mainly your own desire, then reason cannot work and you have to rely on force. Thus, using force is not a sign of strength but rather a sign of weakness. Even in daily human contact, if we talk seriously, using reasons, there is no need to feel anger. We can argue the points. When we fail to prove with reason, then anger comes. When reason ends, then anger begins. Therefore, anger is a sign of weakness.

In this, the second part of my talk, I speak as a Buddhist monk. As a result of more contact with people from other traditions, as time passes I have firmed my conviction that all religions can work together despite fundamental differences in philosophy. Every religion aims at serving humanity. Therefore, it is possible for the various religions to work together to serve humanity and contribute to world peace. So, during these last few years, at every opportunity I try to develop closer relations with other religions.

Buddhism does not accept a theory of God, or a Creator. According to Buddhism, one's own actions are the creator, ultimately. Some people say that, from a certain angle, Buddhism is not a religion but rather a science of mind. Religion has much involvement with faith. Sometimes it seems that there is quite a distance between a way of thinking based on faith and one entirely based on experiment, remaining sceptical. Unless you find something through investigation, you do not want to accept it as fact. From one viewpoint, Buddhism is a religion, from another viewpoint Buddhism is a science of mind and not a religion. Buddhism can be a bridge between these two sides. Therefore, with this conviction I try to have closer ties with scientists, mainly in the fields of cosmology, psychology, neurobiology, physics. In these fields there are insights to share, and to a certain extent we can work together.

Thirdly, I will speak on the Tibetan problem. One of the crucial, serious situations is the Chinese population transfer into Tibet. If the present situation continues for another ten or fifteen years, the Tibetans will be an insignificant minority in their own land, a situation similar to that in inner Mongolia. There the native population is around three million and the Chinese population is around ten million. In East Turkestan, the Chinese population is increasing daily. In Tibet, the native population is six million, whereas the Chinese population is already around seven and one-half million. This is really a serious matter.

In order to develop a closer understanding and harmony between the Chinese and Tibetans—the Chinese call it the unity of the motherland—the first thing necessary to provide the basis for the development of mutual respect is demilitarization, first to limit the number of Chinese soldiers and eventually to remove them altogether. This is crucial. Also, for the purposes of peace in that region, peace and genuine friendship between India and China, the two most populated nations, it is very essential to reduce military forces on both sides of the Himalayan range. For this reason, one point that I have made is that eventually Tibet should be a zone of ahimsa, a zone of non-violence.

Already there are clear indications of nuclear dumping in Tibet and of factories where nuclear weapons are produced. This is a serious matter. Also, there is deforestation, which is very dangerous for the environment. Respect for human rights is also necessary. These are the points I expressed in my Five-Point Peace Plan. These are crucial matters.

We are passing through a most difficult period. I am very encouraged by your warm expression and by the Nobel Peace Prize. I thank you from the depth of my heart.

The interview was over. His Holiness the Dalai Lama sent his secretary, Tenzin Geyche, to get a Tibetan silver coin to present to me as a gift. As we waited alone in the receiving room of his private residence, His Holiness stood, slightly hunched over with hands clasped behind him. I stood near an open window which was framed outside by a bougainvillaea in full bloom, blazing pink in the late afternoon sun. Suddenly His Holiness said to me, "I think this lifetime as Dalai Lama is the most difficult of all the Dalai Lamas." As I let the power of that statement wash over me, feeling the poignancy of it, just as suddenly he looked at me there in front of the radiant window and burst out laughing saying, "Life is so colorful."

14 The Dalai Lama In Depth
Excerpts From An Interview by
Catherine Ingram
(November 2,1988, Dharamsala, India)

CI: Your Holiness, what most influenced you about Gandhi's work?

DL: Many ancient Indian masters have preached nonviolence as a philosophy. That was a more spiritual understanding of it. But Mahatma Gandhi, in this twentieth century, produced a very sophisticated approach because he implemented that very noble philosophy of nonviolence in modern politics, and he succeeded. That is a very great thing.

It has represented an evolutionary leap in political consciousness, his experimentation with truth.

In human society, in the human community, I think the

value of truth is very important. In the early and middle parts of this century, I think many people may have been confused or may have lost respect for truth, because if you have power and money, then truth is something seen as not of much value. I think now we can see that way of thinking is changing. Even the most powerful nations that have everything are seeing that there is no point in neglecting basic human values, basic human faith.

Many places have been totally changed through the use of police force and the power of guns—the Soviet Union, China, Burma, the Philippines, many communist countries, countries in Africa and South America. But eventually, you see, the power of guns and the power of the will of ordinary human beings will change places. I am always telling people that our century is very important historically for the planet. There is a big competition between world peace and world war, between the force of mind and the force of materialism, between democracy and totalitarianism. And now within this century, the force of peace is gaining the upper hand. Still, of course, the material force is very strong, but there is a kind of dissatisfaction about materialism and a realization or feeling that something is missing.

As we are ending this century and entering the twenty-first century, I think the basic concerns are human values and the value of truth. I think these things have more value, more weight now.

This is true in the case of Tibet also. Now it's forty years since the Chinese invasion and we are beginning a new decade. The next twenty years will be another period. Now in this fourth decade, again it's human will—the truth—which is all we have in dealing with China. Despite their brainwashing, despite their using every atrocity and propaganda, and despite all of the resources they have utilized, still the truth remains the truth. Our side has no money, no propaganda, nothing except weak, feeble voices. Yet now most people have lost faith in the strong voices of the Chinese. Their strong voices have lost credibility. Our weak voices have more credibility.

The history of this century is confirming the nonviolence that Mahatma Gandhi and Martin Luther King, Jr., spoke of. Even when it is against a superpower who has all these awful weapons, the reality of the situation can compel the hostile nation to come to terms with nonviolence.

It's a slower process sometimes, but a very effective one.

CI: I was happy to see that your Five-Point Peace Plan had a forceful ecological component to it. Even if we manage not to blow ourselves up with nuclear weapons, or if big countries don't just obliterate smaller countries into extinction, there is an ongoing ecological destruction happening on the planet. Do you forsee the planet surviving this ecological crisis? Do you think we'll make it?

DL: That's difficult to say. I don't know. You see, it is very clear the planet is our own house, and without this we can't survive. That's quite certain. Ultimately, we are the children of the mother Earth, so ultimately we are at the mercy of the mother planet concerning environment and ecology. This is not something sacred or moral. It is a question of our own survival. I think—at least, I hope—that it may not be too late if we realize the importance of the natural environment. In some cases, we may be required to sacrifice some kinds of comfort for a reasonable contentment and therefore treat the natural environment more respectfully. I think it may not be too late, but I don't know. Some scientists today say it is very serious.

CI: A few days after you announced the Five-Point Plan, the Chinese took retaliation against the people in Tibet. Even when you speak out for peace, this kind of thing can happen. Does this make you hesitant to talk about these things publicly? Do you worry about reprisals when you speak about things that may adversely provoke the Chinese?

DL: Actually, you see, the Five-Point proposal was made public, I think at the end of September 1987. Then the Chinese reacted negatively and called me a reactionary. That caused the demonstrations in Tibet, and then the retaliations occurred. So, of course, we were very much concerned and anxious.

You see, on the surface, whether it is very rough or not, there is basically a grave situation in Tibet. I think the Chinese in their way are a very civilized nation. At the same time, they only know force. They do not understand truth. I think now as the time goes, it seems better. There has been a positive change during the last nine years.

Actually the basic content of my Strasbourg proposal [presenting the Five Point Plan to the European Parliament] was already known by the Chinese leaders before the statement was made in the U.S. Our delegation had on one occasion or another explained these basic things to the Chinese government, but they had always neglected our situation and, in some cases, they openly told us, "You are outside of Tibet, and while you remain outside you have no right to make suggestions on these things."

You see, the Chinese are hard of hearing; they are deaf to our voices. As a human being with a human voice, one wants to express or talk to another human being. That's quite logical; it's common sense. But, if there is no listener, then there is no use talking. If there is someone who is willing to listen, then there is more desire to explain. Now in the outside world there are more and more people taking notice of the Tibetan problem. Since our Chinese friends' ears are not so sharp, when we shout loudly it only makes our own voices hoarse. So I make these proposals not in Beijing, but in the outside world. As a result, in the last twelve months the Chinese attitude towards us is more positive than in the past nine years, because of outside world pressure.

CI: But inside Tibet they have been quite repressive.

DL: Yes, for the time being. In the short term, since last year, there has been some setback; it is more rigid. But now I am very glad to know that the Tibetans themselves are very prepared for that fact. So despite the harsh methods of the Chinese, the national determination of the Tibetan people is very strong.

Yesterday I met one young monk who actually participated in the first October demonstration of last year [1987] and who escaped a few days back. I really admired their determination, the ones who participated. But then I asked him, "Do you really feel strong anger toward the Chinese?" and he began weeping, and he said that, yes, he was very angry with the Chinese. And there were some other young children—ten years old, thirteen years old—I met a few months back. One boy who participated in burning some Chinese vehicles had escaped. He also expressed very strong anger. Very sad. Very sad.

CI: So understandable though. Of course, Gandhi and Martin Luther King, Jr., knew that what they were doing sometimes actually provoked violence against them and their people, but they understood that this was necessary to call attention to the situation. Sometimes the nonviolent way may provoke violence.

You have lost very much in this life. You have lost many people who were close to you, and, of course, you have had to deal with the loss of your homeland for these nearly forty years. Do you find a place for grieving in your life? Can you say anything for people who are facing grief—something which we all have to face sooner or later?

DL: There are two ways of losing someone. One is the natural process. I have been a refugee for thirty years. I have lost my mother, teachers, brother. That's nature. Unless old friend disappears, there is no possibility to receive new friend (laughing). So in the same way, as a Buddhist practitioner, one accepts this kind of loss as part of nature. Nothing special. Nothing extraordinary. So there is not much grieving. Of course, for a few days there is some strong feeling of missing someone. But not much effect.

Then there is another category of loss which is due to tragedy, due to disaster. We lost our country, we lost many reliable, good, and spiritual friends, so many friends, lost suddenly and beyond our own control. But in our case, the tragedy began in 1950, so that also is some help. This tragedy has come as a process, and we have become accustomed to it. Much before the actual situation happened, we were already fully convinced that sooner or later, this kind of thing would happen, definitely.

CI: So you expected the worst.

DL: Yes, but of course, sometimes we feel sad. There is more sadness when I hear that many Tibetans, despite their misery and terror, show us so much trust, so much expectation. That gives us some heavy responsibility. That sometimes makes me feel sad. Too much trust, too much expectation is upon us. So little can be done here. There are a lot of limitations. We try our best as much as we can, and as far as possible we have clear motivation. Whether we achieve or not is a different matter.

CI: Do you find that you have a group of people whom you consider your peer group? Are there people with whom you can really relax and just hang out?

DL: Yes, of course. I think generally everybody is my peer group. My attitude is that if somebody is open and straightforward and very sincere, then very easily we can get this close feeling. If someone is very reserved, very formal, then it is difficult. Usually, you see, my nature is very informal. So I think that is helpful.

CI: If you weren't in your position of being the spiritual and temporal leader of Tibet, do you think there would be some other kind of social activism you would undertake, or do you think that you'd prefer to be a monk living quietly in a monastery?

DL: Nowadays, I think, if I were not the Dalai Lama, I would desire time in some monastery or in some remote place to practice deeper meditation. I think in my twenties, thirties, forties, there was a great desire for spiritual practice. These ideas came after contact with Buddha's teachings or as a result of some knowledge about Buddhism. But suppose I still remained in my own place as a farmer, then I don't know. As soon as my birth took place, my father decided that I should enter a monastery, that I should become a monk. But then if those circumstances had been different, most probably I would have become a technician of some kind because I am very interested in mechanical things.

CI: You have spoken about returning to Tibet. Do you think that you will be able to go back to Tibet in this life?

DL: I think so. But this is not a serious matter. The main serious matter is freedom. As we discussed, whether as the Dalai Lama or as a monk, Tenzin Gyatso, I want to have freedom to contribute whatever I can in a maximum way for Tibetans as well as other people. So in that respect, if I feel more opportunity outside Tibet, I will remain outside. If opportunity remains equal, then I will return. Either to Tibet or to China. China is a very beautiful country. And anyway, in the Chinese mind, Buddhism is not alien, not something new. Traditionally there are a lot of Chinese who are Buddhists. There are Buddhist shrines, Buddhist temples, not like in Western countries, where there are only new Buddhist temples and where Buddhism is entirely new. In the Chinese mind, it's not that way. So you see I am quite sure that if the Chinese people have the free opportunity to have contact with Buddhism, to learn and practice Buddhism, I think many young Chinese will have some attraction to it and will benefit. So if such an opportunity happens, of course I am willing to contribute. The Chinese are also human beings.

My real concern is whether something would go wrong with that possibility. No use to return to Tibet or to China if that causes damage or if the opportunity is not there to help.

CI: Do you think there will be another incarnated Dalai Lama?

DL: At the moment is is difficult to say. The next ten or twenty years will determine this. I think Tibetans still want to have a Dalai Lama. Actually, this is not my concern, but if the Tibetan people want to have another Dalai Lama, then the Dalai Lama will come. If circumstances change and the majority of Tibetan people are not much concerned about having a Dalai Lama, then I will be the last Dalai Lama. That is not my responsibility. Those Tibetans who are now age five or ten, it is their responsibility. So in twenty or thirty years when I have passed away, then they will decide.

CI: I hope you will live a long life.

DL: According to my dreams, the maximum years would be 110 or 113. But I could not live that long. So perhaps I will live until I am ninety, between eighty and ninety. Then I would become useless, an old Dalai Lama of not much value.

15 Report from Tibet

"New Crackdown Follows Celebrations in Lhasa"
The Washington Post, *December 21, 1989*

LHASA, Tibet—The awarding of the Nobel Peace Prize to the Dalai Lama, Tibet's exiled spiritual and political leader, has increased tensions between China's Communist rulers and Tibetans and led to a renewed campaign of arrests, surveillance and political reeducation aimed at wiping out nationalist sentiment here, according to Tibetan and Chinese sources.

When news of the award began reaching here over All India Radio after it was announced Oct. 5, Tibetans flocked to holy parks and temples to rejoice and offer prayers of thanksgiving, said the sources, who refused to be identified for fear of government reprisals.

In Lhasa, the religious center of Tibet, hundreds of pilgrims converged on the Norbulinka, the Dalai Lama's former summer palace, to sing, dance and drink barley beer, residents said.

The Dalai Lama headed Tibet's Buddhist theocracy until China forcibly annexed the area in 1950. When Chinese troops suppressed a nationalist uprising in 1959, the Dalai Lama fled to India and formed the Tibetan government in exile. Most of Tibet's monasteries were destroyed over the next twenty years, and nearly all monks were imprisoned or sent to labor camps.

A brief period of liberalization in Communist Party policies in the 1980s unleashed outbreaks of anti-Chinese protests in the region. Between September 1987 and March 1989, security or military forces in Tibet opened fire on non-violent demonstrators at least four times, according to foreign witnesses and Western press reports.

When police opened fire on protesters last March 5, three days of riots followed, according to foreign witnesses and Western press accounts. Medical workers interviewed recently in Lhasa said more than 200 Tibetans were killed—many more than previously reported—by police or troops during the turmoil. Since then, Lhasa, Tibet's capital, has been under martial law.

An estimated 10,000 People's Liberation Army troops now stand sentinel over the city's estimated 50,000 Tibetans, according to a Chinese official with military contacts. Soldiers are camped outside or within striking range of all monasteries, temples and nunneries in the capital, including the Jokhang Temple, the holiest of Tibet's Buddhist temples.

Lhasa's jails now hold more than 680 Tibetans accused of involvement in pro-independence activities, said Tibetans and Chinese officials. Almost half of these are monks, nuns and novices aged thirteen and older. Prison officials routinely employ torture, including beatings and starvation, to extract confessions and information about pro-independence activists, said former detainees interviewed in Lhasa.

Tibetan sources said martial-law troops, most of whom are Chinese and do not speak Tibetan, initially tolerated the festivities honoring the Dalai Lama's Nobel Prize, which was awarded Dec. 10. "We told the soldiers we were celebrating the Tsampa festival—an ancient holiday" that does not exist, said one Lhasan, laughing.

As soon as Communist Party leaders discovered that Tibetans were celebrating the award under the guise of a nonexistent holiday, they ordered a crackdown, said Chinese officials and Tibetans. Troops cleared the summer palace and closed it to Tibetans for three days, said residents.

Authorities launched a search for the organizers of the "secessionist activities," as they labeled the celebration, said several sources, including a Tibet government official. More than 200 Tibetans were detained and interrogated.

The arrests in Lhasa and attacks on the Dalai Lama infuriated Tibetans, triggering a wave of demonstrations calling for an end to Chinese rule in Tibet, said Chinese and Tibetan sources. The demonstrations began in October and despite continuing arrests persisted at least through this month, residents said.

On Dec. 5, a small group of monks gathered at the center of Barkhor Square, where the Jokhang temple is located, the traditional stage of anti-Chinese demonstrations in Lhasa, and shouted, "Long live the Dalai Lama! Tibet for Tibetans!" They were dragged away by armed police, Tibetan witnesses said.

Troops armed with machine guns took up positions in all buildings surrounding the square, including the temple, the witnesses said, and public announcements over loud-speakers warned that troops had been ordered to shoot on sight anyone who joined the "separatist" demonstration, residents said.

Despite the warning, Nobel Peace Prize celebrations and anti-Chinese protests were held in the Tibetan quarter of Lhasa, outside of Barkhor Square, on Dec. 7, 9 and 10, according to Tibetan and foreign sources. "Lhasa is counting down toward an explosion right now," said one Tibetan.

In mid-October six monks chanting "Tibetans want independence" marched to Barkhor Square and shouted demands for an end to Chinese killings of Tibetans and the withdrawal of troops from the region, according to several witnesses. Within minutes, they were taken away by troops, they said. One demonstrator's arms were broken for refusing to identify other pro-independence activists, said sources with police contacts.

At a mass rally held by the Lhasa Public Security Bureau a week later, four of the monks were sentenced to three years of labor reform, without trial, for "attempting to split the motherland," a charge that amounts to treason under Chinese law, according to a report in the Nov. 6 edition of the *Tibet Daily*.

In an effort to eradicate Tibetan nationalism, regional party authorities sent work teams into Lhasa's major monasteries to conduct "reeducation" sessions, Tibetan monks and Chinese officials said.

"Most monks in Lhasa must attend these thought reform classes on a regular basis," said one monk. "Sometimes during the meeting, security officials search the monastery and our living quarters for pro-independence literature and newspapers or tapes containing information about the Dalai Lama."

The party's attempts to police and remold the thoughts of Tibet's Buddhist clergy are not confined to Lhasa. When a foreign tourist group made an unscheduled stop at a monastery in central Tibet, party and military officials were holding an ideological reeducation meeting on the roof of the temple.

16 His Holiness the Dalai Lama's Statement on the Use of the Nobel Peace Prize Money

I have decided to donate a portion of the prize money for the many who are facing starvation in various parts of the world; a portion of it for some of the leprosy programs in India; a portion of it to some existing institutions and programs working for peace; and finally, I would like to use a portion of it as seed money to eventually establish a Tibetan Foundation for Universal Responsibility.

This new foundation will implement projects according to Tibetan Buddhist principles to benefit people everywhere, focusing especially on assisting non-violent methods, on improving communication between religion and science, on securing human rights and democratic freedoms, and on conserving and restoring our precious Mother Earth.

I have deliberately added "Tibetan" to the foundation's name so that this will be one of the first truly Tibetan foundations established to act from the heart of the Tibetan people to do good and helpful things not only for their own country but for people throughout the world.

Old Tibet was a bit too isolated. The future Tibet will be active to help those in need throughout the world, especially using our expertise in psychological, spiritual, and philosophical matters. Of course, many individuals, foundations and governments are already working in these areas, and many more will surely do so as the planetary crisis becomes more obvious and intense. But I believe that our Tibetan combination of spirituality and practicality will make a special contribution, in however modest a way. Once this foundation begins to work we hope to be able to show what a free Tibet can give to the world when its time has come.

Oslo, Norway
December 10, 1989

Source Acknowledgments

Chapt. 1: Nobel Peace Prize Lecture
© His Holiness the Dalai Lama, Tenzin Gyatso
and The Nobel Foundation, Stockholm, Sweden,
1990. Reprinted by permission.

Chapt. 2: Tibet's Living Buddha by Pico Iyer
Iyer, Pico. "Tibet's Living Buddha," *Time Magazine*, April 11, 1988. © 1988 Time Inc. Reprinted
by permission.

Chapt. 3: His Life: An Interview by John Avedon
Avedon, John. "His Life," *An Interview with the
Dalai Lama*. New York: Littlebird Publications,
1980. Adapted and reprinted by permission.

Chapt. 4: A Life in the Day by Vanya Kewley
Kewley, Vanya. "A Life in the Day: The Dalai
Lama," *The London Sunday Times*, Dec. 4, 1988.
© Times Newspapers Ltd., 1988. Reprinted by
permission.

Chapt. 5: Kindness and Compassion
Fred Eppsteiner, ed. "Hope for the Future," *The Path of Compassion: Writings on Socially Engaged Buddhism*, revised second edition. Berkeley: Parallax Press, 1988. Reprinted by permission.

Chapt. 6: Cooperation Among World Religions
An edited compilation from the following sources (see bibliography for full citations):
Dalai Lama och den buddhistiska vägen
Kindness, Clarity and Insight
Meetings in the West
Excerpted and reprinted by permission.

Chapt. 7: Reason, Science and Spiritual Values
An edited compilation from the following sources (see bibliography for full citations):
A Path to Bliss
An Interview with the Dalai Lama
The Bodhgaya Interviews
The Buddhism of Tibet
The Dalai Lama at Harvard
Kindness, Clarity and Insight
Meetings in the West
Adapted and reprinted by permission.

Chapt. 8: Meditation
An edited compilation from the following sources (see bibliography for full citations):
The Bodhgaya Interviews
The Buddhism of Tibet
The Dalai Lama at Harvard
Kindness, Clarity and Insight
Dalai Lama och den buddhistiska vägen
Adapted and reprinted by permission.

Chapt. 9: A Talk to Western Buddhists
An edited compilation from the following sources
(see bibliography for full citations):
The Bodhgaya Interviews
The Buddhism of Tibet
The Dalai Lama at Harvard
Kindness, Clarity and Insight
Dalai Lama och den buddhistiska vägen
Adapted and reprinted by permission.

Chapt. 10: Living Sanely
An edited compilation from the following sources
(see bibliography for full citations):
A Path to Bliss
The Bodhgaya Interviews
The Dalai Lama at Harvard
Kindness, Clarity and Insight
Dalai Lama och den buddhistiska vägen
Adapted and reprinted by permission.

Chapt. 11: Human Rights and Universal Responsibilities
"Universal Responsibilities and Human Rights."
© 1988 The Office of His Holiness the Dalai
Lama. Reprinted by permission.

Chapt. 12: An Ethical Approach to Environmental   Protection
"Humanity and Ecology." © 1988 The Office of
His Holiness the Dalai Lama. Excerpted and
reprinted by permission.

Chapt. 13: The Nobel Evening Address
© His Holiness the Dalai Lama, Tenzin Gyatso
and The Nobel Foundation, Stockholm, Sweden,
1990. This adapted and edited form © Snow Lion
Publications, 1990. Adapted and reprinted by permission.

Bibliography

The Associated Press. "New Crackdown Follows Celebrations in Lhasa", *The Washington Post*, Dec. 21, 1989. © The Associated Press Inc., 1989.

Avedon, John. *An Interview with the Dalai Lama*. New York: Littlebird Publications, 1980.

Bornstein, Anna. *Dalai Lama och den buddhistiska vägen*. Täby,Sweden.: Larsons Förlag, 1988.

Cox, Christine. *Meetings in the West*. Unpublished manuscript. © 1989 Christine Cox

Eppsteiner, Fred, ed., *The Path of Compassion: Writings on Socially Engaged Buddhism*, revised second edition. Berkeley: Parallax Press, 1988.

Goodman, Michael Harris. *The Last Dalai Lama*. Boston: Shambhala Publications, 1986.

Gyatso, Tenzin, Dalai Lama XIV. *A Path to Bliss*. Thupten Jinpa, trans. and ed.; Christine Cox, co-editor. Ithaca, N.Y.: Snow Lion Publications, 1990.

Gyatso, Tenzin, Dalai Lama XIV. *The Bodhgaya Interviews.* José Cabezón, editor. Ithaca, N.Y.: Snow Lion Publications, 1988.

Gyatso, Tenzin, Dalai Lama XIV. *The Buddhism of Tibet.* Jeffrey Hopkins, trans. and editor. Ithaca, N.Y.: Snow Lion Publications, 1987.

Gyatso, Tenzin, Dalai Lama XIV. *The Dalai Lama at Harvard.* Jeffrey Hopkins, trans. and editor. Ithaca, N.Y.: Snow Lion Publications, 1989.

Gyatso, Tenzin, Dalai Lama XIV. *Kindness, Clarity and Insight.* Jeffrey Hopkins, trans. and ed.; Elizabeth Napper, co-editor. Ithaca, N.Y.: Snow Lion Publications, 1984.

Gyatso, Tenzin, Dalai Lama XIV. "The Nobel Evening Address." The Nobel Foundation, Stockholm, Sweden, 1990. © This adapted and edited from © Snow Lion Publications, 1990.

Gyatso, Tenzin, Dalai Lama XIV. "The Nobel Peace Prize Lecture." The Nobel Foundation, Stockholm, Sweden, 1990.

Ingram, Catherine. *In the Footsteps of Gandhi: Conversations with Spiritual Social Activists.* Berkeley: Parallax Press, 1990.

Iyer, Pico. "Tibet's Living Buddha", *Time Magazine,* April 11, 1988.

Kewley, Vanya. "A Life in the Day: The Dalai Lama", *The London Sunday Times,* Dec. 4, 1988.

BOOKS BY HIS HOLINESS THE DALAI LAMA
(Published by Snow Lion Publications)

A Path to Bliss
The Bodhgaya Interviews
The Buddhism of Tibet
The Dalai Lama at Harvard
The Dalai Lama, A Policy of Kindness
Deity Yoga
The Gelug/Kagyu Tradition of Mahamudra
Healing Anger
Kindness, Clarity, and Insight
The Path to Enlightenment
Tantra in Tibet
Transcendent Wisdom
The Union of Bliss and Emptiness

Over 500 books on Tibetan culture—art, adventure, health and medicine, history, language, poetry, philosophy and religion, travel, and women's studies—as well as additional titles by and about the Dalai Lama are available from Snow Lion Publications. Individuals and the trade may **order toll free: 1-800-950-0313.** Catalogs are free upon request. Snow Lion Publications is dedicated to the preservation of Tibetan culture.

Snow Lion Publications
P.O. Box 6483
Ithaca, NY 14851
Tel: 800-950-0313 or 607-273-8519

Announcing the establishment of...

Namgyal Monastery
Institute of Buddhist Studies
The North American Seat of
The Personal Monastery of H.H. the Dalai Lama

In 1992, Namgyal Monastery Institute of Buddhist Studies was founded as a teaching institute and North American seat of Namgyal Monastery, the personal monastery of H.H. the Dalai Lama. The Institute is staffed by Tibetan Buddhist monks and Western scholars and provides an opportunity for the systematic study in English of Tibetan Buddhism in a traditional monastic setting. A wide range of programs are offered including a core 4-year Buddhist Studies Program. All programs are open to both women and men. The Institute is particularly strong in Tibetan language courses. It also offers many special workshops and guest lectures on the arts, debating, meditation, etc. During the summer an Intermediate Colloquial Tibetan Language 6-week Intensive and various retreats are available. The monastery, which is famous for its exquisite sand mandalas, also provides monks for museum and gallery sand mandala exhibitions.

Friends of Namgyal

If you would like to help sustain and develop the North American seat of the personal monastery of H.H. the Dalai Lama and its teaching institute, please contact the monastery at the Ithaca address. You can become a Friend of Namgyal. All donations are tax-deductible. Namgyal Monastery Institute of Buddhist Studies is a registered 501 (c)(3) tax-exempt non-profit organization.

> Namgyal Monastery
> Institute of Buddhist Studies
> P.O. Box 127
> Ithaca, NY 14851

If you would like to be placed on Namgyal's mailing list to receive their periodic newsletters and announcements of courses and special events, please send your name and a donation to cover the expenses of keeping you informed, to the above address.